Yes, We Live in a Mansion

This book is authored by the thirty-six residents listed on a following page. Each of the residents herein have voluntarily shared bits and pieces of their history, knowing that it would be in book form, published, and available for purchase. The goal was to have it in book form before Christmas, and we made it. PTL.

ISBN/SKU 979-8-218-12364-2

This Mansion is a senior independent retirement center. The average age of these residents is in the upper eighties.

"Even to your old age I am he, and to gray hairs I will carry you. I have made, and I will bear; I will carry and will save." Isaiah 46:4 ESV

"Gray hair is a crown of glory; it is gained in a righteous life." Proverbs 16:31 ESV

"Wisdom is with the aged, and understanding in length of days." Job 12:12

"The glory of young men is their strength, but the splendor of old men is their gray hair." Proverbs 20:29 ESV

"You shall stand up before the gray head and honor the face of an old man, and you shall fear your God: I am the Lord." Leviticus 19:32 ESV

"With long life I will satisfy him and show him my salvation." Psalm 91:16 ESV

"So even to old age and gray hairs, O God, do not forsake me, until I proclaim your might to another generation, your power to all those to come." Psalm 71:18 ESV

"Blessed is the one who finds wisdom, and the one who gets understanding," Proverbs 3:13 ESV

"Do not rebuke an older man but encourage him as you would a father, younger men as brothers, older women as mothers, younger women as sisters, in all purity." 1 Timothy 5:1-2 ESV

"So we do not lose heart. Though our outer self is wasting away, our inner self is being renewed day by day." 2 Corinthians 4:16 ESV

"For by me your days will be multiplied, and years will be added to your life." Proverbs 9:11 ESV

"So teach us to number our days that we may get a heart of wisdom." Psalm 90:12 ESV

"I said, 'Let days speak, and many years teach wisdom.' Job 32:7 ESV"

"I remember the days of old; I meditate on all that you have done; I ponder the work of your hands." Psalm 143:5 ESV

This is a book of real stories of some residents here in this mansion. Each resident wrote their own story based on their best memories. Because of my hearing disability, we may have met in our library, and with the help of another resident, I took notes. Some of the residents hand-wrote their short biography, and then I typed it. Some typed it, and I copied it. Each received the first draft, which they could edit, correct, add or delete parts. Then it was redone, and they got an updated copy for their final approval.

For those interested in telling their history, I provided them with a list of suggestions.

Where and when you were born? Birth name. Nationality background?
Brothers and sisters? Any nicknames?
Elementary school. Where? Favorite courses. Anything of interest?
Same with High school. Interests? Sports? Band? Other activities?
College? Grad School? Major, Minor. Activities, Favorite pastime?
First car? First job?

Military service? Branch? Time? Specialty? Where? Significant events.

Married? When? How did you meet? Honeymoon? Where? Children?
Working career experience(s). What, where, and how long?
Vacations? Travels? Where, when. Provide some details. Why there?
Religious affiliation? Yes, No, Why? When?
Retirement experiences. Vacations. Travels. Hobbies?
When did you move into Silver Arrow Estates/Morada?

Please do. Thank you. My goal is to have all these published, printed, and released before Christmas."

Yes, We Live in a Mansion

Robert Adams

I was born in 1932 in Shawnee, Ok. We moved to Tulsa in 1939, when my sister was born. I went to a two-room school house in Seminole, Ok, the first two years.

My elementary school was at Laniel, part of the Tulsa School district. Jr. High for the seventh, eighth, and ninth grades. I just sat in school, not interested in anything. Then to Will Rogers High School and part of the pep club. Graduated 1950. My best friend then was Eddie. I then attended Tulsa U. with a major in Accounting. 2.5 grade average, which was enough to graduate and get into the Phi Epsilon Fraternity the second semester. Flunked out of school to work with dad at the St. Clair building in downtown Tulsa.

In August 1951, I joined the Navy, sent to boot camp in San Diego for six weeks. I was trained in clerical work Yeoman school in San Francisco for six weeks, then shipped out to Guam for eighteen months, working in the Intelligence Office with the FBI.

One day I found files in a secret folder of some 50 to 65 homosexuals in the Navy.

My first car was a 1955 Chevy.

I was sent back to Treasure Island and then to a ship DDE, but did not go. Then, they sent me to the main office mail room.

I quit the Navy in '55. And back to Ok. State in Stillwater to pursue a major in Accounting. I was given a test and aced it. I helped in building a float for the homecoming game, which won first prize. That's when I met the love of my life, as she was working on another float and wanted me to help them. One day, I wanted to kiss her, but she refused and said, "well, I'll see you," and she went home.

We got married in August '59 in Tulsa. We had three kids, two girls, and one boy.

I became a teacher in '61. She was also a teacher of Sixth Grade. I taught Industrial Arts at Clinton Jr. High.

I retired in '84 and bought a fifth wheel, and traveled everywhere, especially in Mexico to Cooper Canyon. There we took a train that had eight flat cars. I had to navigate from one car to another over a homemade bridge held together by men supporting four-by-fours. A guide in front was directing me a bit left or a bit right.

We visited every State Park in Oklahoma that had a golf course. Went to San Antonio, to Brownsville, Texas, and across the border. We went to the city market there in Mexico, where she fell and sprained her ankle. The next day we took a tour bus and then back to the city market.

In Aug 2007, on our fifty-ish anniversary, we took a cruise to Hawaii. Five days to get there, five days touring Hawaii on the main Island, where we took a Helicopter over the Volcano seeing the hot, hot lava flowing down to people's back yards.

We also took a cruise to the Caribbean, to Alaska, and from Ft. Lauderdale to England, Paris, Spain, and Portugal. We enjoyed the local fish and chips with smashed peas at a bar.

Her body was shutting down, and she passed at 6 am 2007.

I moved into Bellarosa, and then to Morada. My son and two grandsons live in Ocoee, near Orlando, Florida.

Charles Allred.

I was born in Alfalfa, Ok, a tiny village southwest of Ok. City on May 28, 1923. I was the third child, one of five.

My parents, Clarence and Ella had a farm where we worked together during the depression. Money was scarce, but the food was plentiful thanks to milk cows, chickens, and their eggs. We had a large garden to maintain, requiring lots of hard work.

My siblings were Hoyt, Willburn, Kenneth, and Joyce. I was called Rusty. We went to a one-room school, which later became part of the Alfalfa school system. My 2nd grade teacher was Pauline Riley, who would later become my mother-in-law.

My first job was farm work for a neighbor who worked for the county road crew. My first car was a '31 Chevy convertible, which my uncle found and restored it in good working condition, giving it a new paint job. It was my dream car.

In 1943, I joined the Navy, and eventually assigned to the USS Amycus. a landing ship tank (LST) we nicknamed Low Ship Target. It was converted to a repair ship, where I served in the Pacific theater. While there, we were hit during a battle, and I was injured by shrapnel. I found out later that I was the most seriously injured survivor.

I met my future wife, Marilyn Riley, in her hometown. My favorite story is when she was sitting on the sidewalk and flipped off her sandals so she could flip sand with her toes. We dated a couple of years when I was home on leave, and after my discharge, we became engaged. We were married on August 13, 1947, and will celebrate our 75th wedding anniversary this year.

We've been blessed with two children: Cheryl Smith (now deceased) and Terry Gene, who served his country during the Vietnam conflict and now resides in McLoud, Ok. We now have six grandchildren, ten great-grandchildren, and three great, great-grandkids. Oh, what a blessing it's been.

In 1948, I began working at Tinker Air force Base, SE of Oklahoma City as a jet engine technician of parts for airplanes at Tinker, which was the prime maintenance and repair location.

I retired in 1977.

After our children were on their own, Marilyn and I began RV-ing. We have traveled from the Atlantic to the Pacific. From the Mexican border to Canada, making many friends along the way. Much of our traveling was spent meeting and traveling with Nelson and Mary Aurich. He was a shipmate of mine, and since we were Okies, we bonded as family.

I spent many, perhaps as many as ten years volunteering at the Wagoner Community Hospital. I have served on the Benevolent committee at the First Baptist Church in Wagoner.

We moved to Silver Arrow Estates, now named Morada, in 2015.

Marilyn Allred.

I was born at my maternal grandparents' home in the community of Cloud Chief, Ok, on January 25, 1930, during a blizzard, I'd been told. That blizzard still holds record conditions. My parents, Clauda and Pauline Riley were pioneer school teachers in Caddo County. We moved frequently to better my parents chances of promotions.

My brother, Carl Claude was born in 1939, and boy did he change things. He was always exploring and wondering how things work. He was killed in a car wreck in July 1969.

In 1944, we moved from Binger to Eakly, Ok, just 14 miles west.

In that small high school, my main interest was in sports, softball, and basketball, along with other activities and favorite subjects like biology, science, and history. I always felt that being raised in a small town and attending a small school gave me a sense of grounding and what is important in life.

Charles and I met in my hometown when a girl friend and I were just hanging out. I saw this handsome sailor and thought he was cute. We dated when he came home on leave, and became engaged during my senior high school year. The rest is history.

We've been blessed with two children: Cheryl Smith (deceased) and Terry Gene, who also served his country during the Vietnam conflict, and now resides in McLoud, Ok. And now we have six grandchildren, ten great-grandkids, and three great, great, grandchildren. Five generations to be proud of.

After Charles and I were married, my first full-time job was working in a real estate and insurance office in Anadarko, Ok.

Charles and I both worked at Tinker Air force Base as civilian employees. I worked intermittently for twenty-one years. He retired after 30 years.

Following my retirement, I decided to follow my heart by making porcelain dolls. We sold some to make room for more, and soon began doing craft shows. There we met many nice people as customers and fellow crafters.

Then back to RVing all over the US, from the east coast to the west coast, from the Florida Key West to Seattle meeting many fellow RVers in those campsites who became friends. We loved that life style.

Finally, we moved into Silver Arrow Estates in 2015 after twenty years in the Ft. Gibson Lake area and the town of Wagoner. It's been a great life.

Serafina Ann Barbaro

Call me Sara. I was born in 1934 in Long Beach (Long Island) New York. My parents are from southern Italy in a town called Molfetta. After they married and were searching for a better life, they packed all their worldly belongings and boarded a ship bound for America!

My Dad, Vincent Breglia, owned and operated a fish market, while mom (Antonia) took care of us, my older brother Nicolas and a younger sister Janet. Unfortunately, Nicolas drowned in his sixth year. My nickname then was Dusty. We had a happy family. I fondly remember making wine with my Father and getting a bike for Christmas. Mom was a role model for me.

During that 2nd World War, a special memory was seeing the flags in the windows for the soldiers who went off to war.

As a young girl, beginning in grammar school, Jr. High, and all through Long Beach High School, I enjoyed English and Art classes, was a Drum Majorette, leading the marching band in many parades, twirling my baton! For more fun, I sang in the choir.

After twirling my way through high school, I graduated from Brown's Business College and soon began my secretarial career at an insurance company and then with Paramount Pictures as a film distributor, and then onto CBS.

I met John while in high school. We met at a dance on a Sunday afternoon! His best compliment was that I'm very helpful! He had enlisted in the Army and was on his way to Germany. After writing daily letters for a year, we married upon his return on May 3, 1959, and went to Cuba for our honeymoon. We had many wonderful years raising our three Children, John, Jean, and Laura. Caring for and loving them was happiness to me. I sewed their clothes as they were needed and grew into larger sizes. I learned to drive a stick shift in a 1947 black Chevy Fleetline.

After some thirty years, John retired from Met Life in New York City, when we joined a travel group and started to travel around the world: to Switzerland, Holland, Greece, Italy, Canada, Turkey, Denmark, France, Norway, Poland, Russia, Venezuela, and Germany.

I was asked if I was a warning label, what would it say? Watch your mouth or else!

Carolyn Bollingsley.

I was born on March 15, 1938, in Wichita, Kansas.

When I was two years old, we moved to Santa Catalina Island, off the coast of Southern California, south-southwest of Long Beach. My dad was in the Navy, part of the <u>maritime service.</u>

In elementary school in Salina, CA. for first through fifth grade, and then we moved to Oregon. My Parents had leashed a restaurant where Dad cooked, and Mom waited on customers. I remember a parade the school held in that main street in Salina in 1945. We rode bikes to help celebrate the war's end when Germany surrendered.

I have a half-sister, my father died when I was nine years old, and we moved to Ponca City, OK.

Played the piano.

In Ponca City, I played the drums in High school.

I was diagnosed with Pollio when I was twelve years old, and over time, I had four spinal surgeries leaving me severely handicapped, but I did not give in. Mom and Dad told me I could not play the drums in the school band. I spent many hours for two years in the bedroom learning to play the clarinet, so I could be in the band. In High School, I won the position of first clarinet to be the band queen. So, I got to march.

I got married in 1956 to a friend I met at a HS football game. When I graduated we got married. Had two girls and one boy. First husband died.

Went with the band to the tri-state festival in Enid. Oh, there was a carnival there with all those rides. I was told I could not ride because of my disability. But I went anyway. That determination to go would not keep me confined. A very lucky Polio patient.

My favorite subjects were English and Music. In summer school, I insisted I can do it.

My second husband was an ophthalmologist, eye surgeon and a teacher of the practice. We had five kids together, my son and his four kids. He got his medical degree in 1956, at the age of '26. The Navy assigned him to Claremore, Ok. to the Native Indian hospital ministering to them as an ophthalmologist for thirty years.

After his retirement, we cruised to England, Finland and Russia.

I have been a member of the Church of Christ for nine years in Ponca City, the same church my grandmother attended. Spent ½ year in Ardmore and moved to Broken Arrow, where three of my kids live. Moved into Silver Arrow Estates/Morada in 2017. My husband died two years later in 2019, of a massive stroke, and he died shortly after.

He lived for 87 wonderful years.

Salvatore Brucculeri.

This is my story. Please call me Sam.

I was born on October 1, 1935, in Sicily, the largest Island off the toe of Italy's boot.

As a kid, we would throw fruit to the American soldiers as their train passed. They would then toss candy and cigarettes to us. I fondly remember Germany surrendering on May 7, 1945, when I was just nine years old.

My father passed away in January 1946, and my mother continually cared for and raised me and my sibling. She was encouraged to come to America to avoid the aftermath of WW11.

At eleven years old, I wanted to quit school and go to work. My mother said No. In June, I graduated with a fifth-grade certificate, which is equal to a high school diploma here in America.

I started to work watching cows from five in the morning until ten, when the cows are put in the barn till about three or four that afternoon. Time to go back into the field as it was cooler. At about eight, we'd bring the cows back to the barn to milk them and let them rest until four in the morning.

I applied to college for the priesthood, which was free since I was an orphan. In Sept, I quit my job as we had to return to school. In October, the lady representing the priesthood college informed my mother that the classes had already started. She then suggested that I go to a trade school, which was out of town. My mother said, "no, he can learn a trade here in town." I went back to watching the cows and sheep.

When I was sixteen, my mother received a letter from my uncle in the US suggesting that I come to America to work. The American Council told my uncle he could get a visa for direct family members; sisters, brothers, mother, father, etc. but not for a nephew. He applied for all of us. Over the next four years, nothing. No calls. No word. We learned our name had been mis-spelled.

My grandmother's brother living in Indiana, or Pennsylvania, came to Italy for a visit. He asked my mother what happened. Mom told him we had not been contacted by the American council. The next day he went there, and got the name spelling corrected. The council then informed my mother that she can take children under twenty-one. I had two older sisters, one married and going to Belgium with her husband. This was in the first part of July. I was concerned about leaving my other sister alone, so that night lying down on my bed looking at the ceiling, I said, "God, if you are a real god the way people say you are, you could do this. Either my sister gets married, and she goes with us, or none of us go. I do not want my sister to be alone."

In August, she got engaged, married on September 6, and left for France on the ninth. My mother, younger sister, and I took a ship to America and, passing the Statute of Liberty, landed in the New York Port on September 20. I got seasick.

We then stayed with my Uncle Dick in Jamestown, NY. On Sunday, he said, "if you want to go to the Catholic Church," he pointed to it up the street. "But if you want to go with me, I will take you to the Pentecostal Church." I said we're no longer Catholic but Pentecostal. After two weeks, I started work with my uncle. Two years later, everyone got laid off as they closed the shop. I then started working in different factories.

In July 1960, I married Maria.

In 1961, I became an American citizen, and learning to speak English was a BIG accomplishment for me. Our son Jeff was born in 1965. I worked for several years in furniture factories, and then I hurt my back.

My first car was a 1952 Plymouth, for which I paid $300, and sold it a year later for $300.

In Nov 1969, I decided to attend Barber School in Buffalo, NY, and got certified in May 1970. I started to work for two barbers in Lakewood. After June 1971, I purchased a shop on Second St. Jamestown, NY. Times were tough, and people did not get haircuts. I talked with my wife about purchasing an old house across the street from my shop. We sold the house we were living in. With the money we received, the mortgage was paid, and the old house was paid for in cash. In 1976, I took a job for the school system to help pay for our living expenses. In 1980 Maria passed away.

I met Ruth the following year. Yes, now married for forty-two years.

A favorite Bible verse is John 3:16 since I was saved in Italy at the age of twenty.

The thing that influenced me the most while growing up was my cousin Stephen, and my grandfather Filippo in Italy. Sometimes for the good, and sometimes for the not-so-good. A special gift was a watch my aunt gave me when I left Italy. I still have it.

Next question. Was it love at first sight when I met Ruth? She wrote a letter to God asking Him for a spirit-filled Christian with brown eyes and light hair. She knows God sent me to her.

And here's the last. I would like to be remembered as humble, hard-working, and willing to help others, and I love God and family very much.

Antoinette Renee Brunson

I was born n January 24, 1949, in Stockton, California. I'm of Irish, Scottish, Cherokee, and English descent.

Toni was and still is my nickname.

I was blessed with three sisters; Reta and Claudia, and Robin. No brothers.

My favorite subjects in elementary school were Reading and writing, but the one I favored most was history. It was the same in High School, along with language study in French. I enjoyed playing basketball and softball. I went to the University of California in Davis with major studies in Social Science, History and minors in Humanities and English. I Graduated on June 15, 1971, and got the state standard teaching credentials. A favorite pastime was reading history.

My first car was a Studebaker.

My first job was working for the California State collecting unpaid taxes from residents for three years and then promoted to a higher level.

In 1975, I enlisted in the 124th army reserve command at Fort Lawton, Washington. Company D Engineer Battalion. I was a supply clerk for the engineer unit specialist 4th class. In those years, I won six medals.

1. Army achievement medal, 1985 Seargent Antonette Dickey.

2. Army achievement metal First Oak Leaf Cluster 1985.

3. Army Commendation Medal Staff Seargent Dickey 1988.

4. The Commendation medal Seargent Dickey First Class 1993

5. Chief Intel Operations Seargent Dickey 1995.

6. The Meritorious Service Medal First Seargent Dickey Class 1995.

Michael Wayne Dickey and I worked in the same building with frequent interactions. We married in 1980. We divorced two and a half years later as he became an alcoholic.

I've done some traveling to places in Arizona to visit family. Before my divorce, we went down the coast to southern California and visited Disneyland, and also to Ireland to visit my ancestral country.

Two years before my army retirement in 1995, a new member joined our unit, and she began to tell me things about God, Jesus, and church. That led to me visiting and becoming a member of a church. I volunteered a great deal and went to work for the church. The pastors were Rhema graduates, and after those years in Sacramento, I moved to Oklahoma, enrolled in the Bible School for two years, and then returned to California, back to the same church to volunteer.

But, I needed a paying job and got work with Paychex, a payroll company, and a bit later was transferred to an office in Albuquerque, New Mexico. I fell in love with the area, and there was a Rhema church there too. I enjoyed traveling throughout New Mexico. After being on staff with Paychex for four years, I retired from that and moved back to Oklahoma to return to Rhema Bible College.

I still enjoy reading and studying history, having moved into Morada in June 2022.

Jay Bullard

**How a Boy from The Missouri
Ozarks Became a Methodist
Medical Missionary in Africa.**

Today as I am on the threshold of my 8th decade of life, I'm looking back over the years, wondering how in the world did it ever happen that 1 was a Methodist Medical Missionary in Africa? It really did happen, and those three years in Africa are undoubtedly the most influential, instructional, defining, and guiding of my life. From the minute I first set foot in Africa until this very instant, my life has been "shaped" by my African experience. Sure, my wife, kids, and grandkids have had an important loving effect on my life, but that is a different realm from my African experience.

This writing aims to analyze how a country boy from the Ozark Mountain got to a little hospital in the mountains of Algeria, North Africa, as a medical missionary. It is an attempt to explain just how did it happen!

Perhaps, the "die was cast," and I took my first step on the path towards Africa on that early spring day in 1967. I was at Fort Benning, Georgia. I had enlisted in the Army and was training to be a 2nd Lieutenant Infantry Platoon leader in Vietnam. That particular day my company was doing training involving napalm. The Air Force dropped napalm far enough away from us so that no one could be hurt but close enough so we could experience the heat and smell. Prior to that moment, my year's infantry training had just been fun and games. When that heat and smell of hot kerosene "rolled" over me, I suddenly realized someone could get hurt. That stuff could kill people!

"Wait a minute!" I don't want to kill anybody; I don't want to be responsible for getting somebody killed! Why was I training to go to Vietnam, where I had no idea where it was, to kill people for some reason that I did not understand!

Anyway, at that moment, I prayed! In summary, my prayer was, "GOD, get me out of this mess I have gotten myself into, and I will become a preacher!"

Maybe I should back up a bit to explain how I had gotten into such a dire predicament that I felt it necessary to attempt to bribe GOD! I had gone through my whole childhood, elementary school, middle school, high school, and college as a lazy C- or D+ student with no ambition, goals, or life plan. When I graduated college, 1 had no desire to work or do much of anything, so l enlisted in the Army.

Back in the second half of the 4th year of the five years, it took me to get a 4-year college degree, I met Judith Carmen Ford. We graduated college together.

While I was in infantry training and Judy was in her first year of Graduate School, we became engaged. We planned to get married in June 1967, just before I left for Vietnam.

Back to that day when I was first experiencing the wonders of napalm, just before the heat and smell reached me, the only significant thing in my life was my relationship with Judy. I don't know how much she was in my thinking then, but when the heat and smell arrived, I made what I hoped would be an offer to GOD he could not refuse. Everything changed. At that instant, I quit the Army!

The Army was not happy when I told them I quit! They had spent a year training me to use the various infantry tools, everything from bayonets to bazookas. I had shot up over $100,000 worth of ammo. I knew what my punishment would be; Vietnam, here I come, as a light weapons infantryman (11B10). However, a week later, when I got my new orders, I could not believe it. As my "punishment," the Army transferred me out of the Infantry into the Medical Corp, and instead of Vietnam, they sent me to Germany. And, instead of my 3-year enlistment, I got a two-year "hitch" just like a draftee. So, Judy and I got married, and we went to Europe for a year-long honeymoon on Uncle Sam!

My orders sending me to Germany was to be a Medical Lab Specialist; I had no earthly idea what that was or what I was supposed to do. So, I spent the second year of my military career learning and getting a lot of practical experience working in a medical lab. Sometime during our year in Europe, Judy and I came up with the idea that since we were serving our country in the military, maybe after the military, we should do something to serve God.

We contacted both the Presbyterian and the Methodist Mission Boards to see if they could use us in some way. The Methodist expressed a luke-warm interest in us to possibly become Methodist missionaries, most likely because Judy had been working on her master's degree in Christian education.

But then, my enlistment ended, and the Army said we could go home, so we did. We returned to Missouri, got good jobs, bought a new mobile home, and settled down to Live the "good life" in America. Judy was the youth director at the YWCA.

Since I had a weak degree in biology and a minor in chemistry, I was able to get a job as a Quality Control/Method Development Chemist at a veterinarian pharmaceutical company. It was a really good job, interesting work, and I learned lots of new procedures. I could have been happy there for years.

However, we stayed in touch with the Methodist Mission Board, and they "dangled" the possibility of my being a medical technologist missionary in Vietnam. The Methodists were serious enough to have Judy, and I undergo an interview process. The interviewers decided that Judy was stable and Methodist enough to be a missionary, but I needed some work. The Methodist Mission Board recommended that I have some psychological work and that I needed to be a registered medical technologist before I could become a Methodist missionary.

To become a registered medical technologist (MT ASCP), I needed to do a one-year internship training at a teaching hospital. So, I quit my really good chemist job and enrolled in the medical technology program at Menorah Medical Center, the Jewish hospital in Kansas City, Missouri. I did my year internship at a Jewish hospital. The Methodist Mission Board was correct. I needed that training to be an effective medical technologist on the mission field, and that year's training has been extremely important throughout the rest of my life.

Now about the psychological business, I thought that it was a crazy idea. However, looking back over my life, I realize the Board was also right about I being able to benefit from some psychological re-adjustment. It seemed crazy at the time, but the Board sent me to talk to a psychiatrist.

The psychiatrist wore black and white wingtip shoes like my Uncle Lee. In fact, he looked a lot like my Uncle Lee. I loved my Uncle Lee, but I would never have told Uncle Lee about my deep interpersonal feelings, so I wasn't going to tell the psychiatrist either. Well, as a result, I had to go thru a weeklong intensive psychoanalysis session. At the time, I thought it a major waste of time, but the basis of the sessions was a psychological theory popular at that time called 'Transactional Analysis!'. In spite of myself, I learned some concepts that have been important and useful throughout my life that still influence my thinking today about my concepts of life, religion, and GOD.

Well, I finished my training and became a full-fledged registered medical technologist and had some psychotherapy and thereby met the requirements of the Methodist Mission Board. However, by that time, the mission field in Vietnam had closed, and there were no other openings with Methodist Missions for a medical technologist. So, I took a job as a Med Tech at a small hospital in Neosho, Missouri.

We enjoyed Neosho. It is a small town in Southwest Missouri, known as the flowerbox city because of all the pretty little flower boxes on the town square. Judy's brother and his family lived there, and that was one reason we had decided to settle in Neosho. We rented a cute little house within walking distance of the hospital. The work at the hospital was interesting and enjoyable, and I felt it was significantly important. Our first child, our son, was born there. We started to look for a house to buy to settle down for the long term. We had just about decided on a pretty little place with a few acres in the county as a place to settle down and raise a family.

But then one day, out of the blue, The Methodist Mission Board called, and they had an urgent need for a Med. Tech. in Algeria, North Africa. They gave us 24 hours to decide whether we would go or not. We call that our "Call" from God, and that He must live at 475 Riverside Drive, New York, since that is where the call originated. Obviously, we decided to go.

We left Neosho, Missouri, June, 1971 and went for missionary orientation for 2.5 months in Stoney Point, New York. Then to Le Chambon-sur-Lignon, France, for five months of French language training, then across the Mediterranean to Tunis, Tunisia, North Africa, for a month of orientation to Muslim North Africa. And we finally arrived on March 3, 1972, at Il Maten, Algeria, North Africa.

When we arrived at Il Maten, Algeria, North Africa, I had no idea I was about to start an adventure that would shape, direct and define the rest of my life. All my life since that time in Algeria has been influenced by that experience in some way or another.

Looking back now, I wonder, did God and I actually establish a covenant there at the napalm training range in Fort Benning Georgia? I did not become a preacher, but I was a missionary and have done a little "preaching" at times, and it was almost miraculous how I got out of the mess I was in so that I went to a lab in Germany instead of a battlefield in Vietnam? Or as an alternate possibility is that I was, and still am, just stumbling through life with no set direction or purpose, and it is just random chance that I passed thru Africa and stumbled through my overly blessed life that followed? Or is it that God had a plan for my life, and I have just been living out the pre-set drama? Or is it as I believe that GOD "gives" us opportunities in life to experience GOD.

We have free will to accept or not to accept these opportunities, it is not a "sin" to not take the opportunity, but it is a blessing to take the opportunity to experience GOD. I believe experiencing GOD is life's greatest adventure, and experiencing GOD is what gives life meaning.

I thank GOD for the opportunity to experience life as a Methodist medical missionary there in Muslim North Africa!

Judy Bullard

Memories for hope

On the second day of Christmas (December 26)

A Diaper Miracle.

One of the problems that young mothers on the mission field have is keeping diapers and clothes clean for their babies. When there was enough rain, there was enough water in the well to keep the water pipes in the house producing water. When there was no rain for a while, the wells would get low, and we had to crawl down into the well to reach the water with a bucket. Incredibly, we had two washing machines on the mission station we could use when there was enough water. We hung the clothes out on a clothesline to dry.

One August, the shortage of rain meant there was little water to wash diapers. I got one bucket to wash them in and one to rinse. Needless to say, Jamie had a diaper rash. We kept praying for rain, but God had another miracle in mind.

When we were in the States, we used Baby Scott's

disposable diapers. There was a plastic panti that came with them. The diaper fit inside the panti, and we still had the outer panti. We had long since run out of disposable diapers. One day the hospital got some new medical equipment from the United States. When they were unwrapped, low and behold, the equipment was wrapped in Baby Scotts disposable diapers. There was enough to almost make it until the rains came!

Praise the Lord!

Labour Wisdom

When I worked at the Tulsa Convention and Visitors Bureau, I answered the phone lines. Many of the questions had to do with what there was to see and do in Tulsa. I also got the question, "where can I see Indians, where are their reservations?" I enjoyed telling them that we had no reservations. The Indians all got their allotted land in 1887-1900 and own their property. Just walk down almost any street in Tulsa, and you will meet someone who is part Indian (Native American).

For 30-40 years I worked out in the world in various jobs trying to make the world a better place to live and to supplement my family income.

After we came back from the Philippines, we settled in the Tulsa area. The older two children were in school all day, and Julieta was in preschool. We needed extra money, so I tried my hand at Life Insurance sales and developed a business selling vitamins and Shaklee Corporation household products. I could do this part-time out of my home. Later I worked full-time as an appointment clerk at ORU and the City of Faith. Jay worked at the University also, so we could ride together.

Most of the work I did was secretarial, working with patients and doctors. During this time, I realized I needed more experience working with computers and began taking classes at Tulsa Technology School. One time I worked as an administrative secretary at the Frances Willard Home for Girls, the Tulsa Chamber of Commerce in the Convention and the Visitors Bureau, and then at the OSU School of Medicine in the Family Medicine department working with the 4th year medical students. I scheduled lectures for them to hear before they started their clinical rounds. Jay and I still work with medical students being Senior Mentors. The second-year students practice interviewing skills three times a year. We try to teach them to speak loud and slowly.

With all this experience working with people and their schedules, what did I learn?

There are twelve things that I learned over the years. They are in no order of importance:

1. Computer skills are necessary.
2. Accurate records are important, so keep hard copies as computers can go down.
3. Always do a follow-up to confirm the time and date of speakers.

4. Proofread all typed materials.

5. Youth and adults learn best by doing.

6. Ask fellow workers and group members for their ideas of what is important to them when working on a group project

7. People are busy. get to the point

8. Start on time and end on time.

9. Accidents and reschedules will happen.

10. Plan ahead for number 9.

11. Family is important. Plan time for them.

12. Show love and respect in all relationships and be
sensitive to·their feelings, especially workers.

I also learned that men rely on their secretaries and wives to keep them aware of their daily schedules. If they are wise, they will marry someone who can do this.

Thank you. Lord, for teaching me these skills throughout my life.

Carol Lou Allen Canning

I was born November 10, 1936 in Tolleson, Arizona to Ellen and Ez Allen. Our ancestors were of English and American Indian descent. I was the middle child between my brother, Ezekiel Earl and sister Rita Jo. Both are still living. My brother lives in Bergheim, Tx, just outside San Antonio. Rita Jo in Oklahoma City.

I grew up in the Church of Christ, where my grandpa on my mother's side was a pastor and farmer. He traveled by horse to preach around the county and was paid with crops or meat. Grandpa Spencer passed away in the spring of 1950 at age 89. I was fourteen.

I am eternally grateful for those early memories and my belief in Christ as the Son of God at an early age.

I attended elementary school in Tolleson, Az., till the fourth grade when we moved to Oklahoma City. My favorite subjects were reading and spelling. The best incentive to be a good speller was a chocolate bar awarded to the student left standing at the end of each spelling bee.

There was one part of my elementary school years that was very difficult. At the age of nine, my doctor sent me to bed due to complications of pneumonia scaring on my lungs. Tuberculosis was rampant at the time, and bedrest was a precautionary measure to keep me from contracting TB.

Just imagine a nine-year-old girl entertaining herself while bedridden for nine months! I got to exercise my creative talents by making finger puppets from orange skins, and I developed my love of singing which has continued into adulthood.

The doctor finally relented when TB had not developed and let me return to school after missing almost the entire year. By fourth grade, we moved to Oklahoma City.

Jackson Jr. High school (7th to 9th grade) was within walking distance of my home. Capital Hill Senior High School was far enough away that I had to ride the bus. My favorite subjects were sewing and typing. I loved being part of the Pep Club, supporting our winning teams all three years.

I met my husband, Harry Canning on a blind date in my senior year. We eloped.

I finished high school and then worked as a painting company secretary until I became pregnant with our first child. Harry was a commercial sheet metal worker, and also in the Air Force Reserves as a medic. I was a stay at home mom of two girls and a boy until my youngest entered 5th grade. At that time, I went to work at my kid's school and, for the next ten years, did many office jobs, including secretary to the assistant principal.

While the kids were growing up, we spent vacations in our camper exploring the Western US, and the provinces of Canada. Exploring the Eastern US, the kids particularly enjoyed Worlds of Fun in Orlando, Florida, a Walt Disney theme park.

The whole family loved the weekends and summers spent at our cabin at Grand Lake near Grove and Jay, Oklahoma.

My love for singing, born in my childhood years, continued throughout my years in Oklahoma City, where I was a member of a performing group called The Treble Clefs. I continue to enjoy singing as a member of the Silver Tones Choir here at Morada.

For eight years after the kids were grown, Harry and I took part in re-enactments of the Civil War and Indian Wars and made many lasting friends at these events in Guthrie, Ok.

My husband of sixty-five years passed away in 2019, and that is when I came to Silver Arrow Estates, now Morada.

I love it here and plan to stay till God takes me home.

Reba Ann Chronister

I Was born as Reba Ann Scantling in the small town of Heavener, Ok, not far from Ft. Smith, Arkansas, on Feb. 9, 1936, and birthed in our home, not a hospital. I was number six of four brothers and three sisters. Dad worked for the Kansas City railroad, while mom raised and cared for us. His heritage goes back to Ireland and the Cherokee tribe that eventually made their way to the states. I've got a pamphlet detailing their historical movements.

Back in the late thirties, the agricultural town of Heavener consisted of a post office/store, the railroad, a sawmill, and charcoal mining, with the homes scattered around, but yet a population of around two thousand.

Heavener was big enough that the local elementary school had enough students for each grade, except kindergarten, who sat in the first row with the first-grade students behind those. When I was about eight, whoever of my bros and sis got to the bikes first rode them, and of course, they were boys bikes.

I loved to sing and dance, so in High School, I was part of the glee club and the pep club at football games. Classes then included learning to sew in Home Ec, cooking, typing, and book keeping. But my role model was aunt Lou, who taught me how to cook. The sweet sixteens was when I was ready to take on the world after enjoying the milking of cows and gathering eggs. Somewhere in those days, I got a dog we named Lucky because he found a home. With all that, I would always remember the Pearl Harbor attack in 1941.

I was still in HS when I met Isom Lee Chronister when he had been transferred from another school district to ours. We dated a few years and married in 1956. He was a radio operator, then worked in electronics getting a job with Rock Island Railroad in Iowa. When we moved back to Tulsa, he worked for American Air Lines as an Electronic Technician. I had four children, for which I would say raising and caring for them was my greatest achievement. And now I have ten grandchildren, sixteen great-grandchildren, and one great-great-great grandchild on the way as of Sept 2022.

Through all those years, we attended churches in the area where we were living. But my fondest time was being Baptised in a small town baptist church in Mazie, Oklahoma, just south of Chouteau, at the age of 82. Never will I forget it. I also started taking piano lessons at eighty-two.

When the kids were out of school, I worked in a school kitchen and then for a sewing factory in Prior Ok.

After Lee retired from American Air Lines we did some traveling around the country. To California, to Chicago where he had a half-brother. But the greatest was to visit and see Hawaii and enjoy those beaches twirling around the wonderfully soft sandy beaches with the approaching waves.

He passed in 2017, and I moved to Broken Arrow into Silver Arrow Estates, now named Morada, four years ago.

I was recently asked, "What is necessary to live a good life?" I replied: "to be a Christian and be available to do God's work."

A few months ago, in June this year, I had a dream. I was in the most beautiful garden of all, and there in front of me, I saw Jesus with His arms out ready to accept me. I took a step or two toward Him, and then suddenly he disappeared. I woke up crying and still do when I think about it.

"The Lord is my Shephard, I shall not want..." Psalm 23.

Nate Clark.

I was born in 1927 in Ponca City, Ok.

Oh, in high school, I got a nickname. "You're a Nate," which turned into "Urinate." My mother frowned at it, but what can you do when all the athletes use it, and you are a wimp.?

In the late '20s, my father was the treasure of the Marland Oil Company, thus a well-paying job. However, J.P. Morgan took over Marland about 1929 and turned it over to a small oil company called Continental Oil. The result for Marland Oil was to become a major oil company (Conoco)., and my father became jobless. While I knew some wealth early in my life, the result was that my father was somewhat soured, which impacted my companionship with him. We had difficulty with our relationship in the later years.

We lived roughly five hundred yards from the estate of E.W. Marland, later to become the Governor of the state. His property was several square miles in area, and he turned it into a game preserve.

Starting around the age of twelve or so, five or six other boys my age and I would sneak into the preserve, swim and fish in a lake with the turtles, snakes, frogs, etc. We built huts of sticks and grass, smoked grapevine, and became close friends. The caretaker of Marland was named Karl. It was our understanding that he was brought to this country as a prisoner-of-war from the WW1 German Army. This made his efforts to keep us off the estate all the more exciting. My brother and I are the only ones left from this close group.

I graduated from high school in June 1945. I then joined the U.S. Navy and was assigned to a mine sweeper that had a wooden hull. This makes them less attractive to magnetic mines than a vessel with an iron hull. We were sent to the Inland Sea of Japan to sweep, but mines either were not there, or had gone sterile. However, the devastation of Japan from our bombing was n horrible. We were the first Americans sent to the harbors of Japan, which had to be declared "mine safe" before other ships could be docked there.

In the spring of 1946, we left Japan to go to San Francisco, but on the way, we ran into a colossal typhoon south of Okinawa for about four days. Wow! That wooden hull creaked and groaned as the waves were higher than the mast of our small (136' long) vessel. But it held together, and we made it. I was discharged in Norman, Ok. in August 1946.

I started college at Oklahoma University with a major in petroleum engineering. I am not much of a scholar, and the difficult curriculum made it awhile to graduate with an engineering degree in the Spring of 1952. In the meantime, I waited tables and lived in the basement of a sorority house where I was a houseboy. This was truly a good job, and I got room and board as a college attendee.

After graduation, I was employed by a Tulsa company, Helmerich & Payne, and soon married a beautiful girl (Beverly). We lived and worked in towns of Oklahoma and Kansas. During this period, two girls followed by two boys were born. I worked in an office and on wells in the field during this period. In 1962 we were transferred to Tulsa.

In Tulsa, I did engineering work in the office. But when a drilling or producing well was in trouble, I was assigned to go to the field and stay there day and night until the problem was solved. One particularly difficult well to fix was the "State 1 – 10" in western Oklahoma. It was a high-pressure, high-volume blowout. This is where I met Coots Andrews of Boots and Coots, blowout specialists. We had this well turned down the line in twenty days. A well-done achievement.

As time went on, both the engineering and field work became more challenging. A change in supervision at the company's vice presidential level was not to my liking. I felt that a heart attack, a stroke, or a nervous breakdown was in the offering, so I retired in 1978.

By the end of my career, all of our children had graduated from a four-year college, one with a master's degree in Electrical Engineering from Cal Tech. We lost our oldest, a beautiful daughter, about twenty years ago.

After retirement, we were able to travel. We have been to six continents. We found <u>Elderhostel</u>, short courses on various subjects of great interest, and have attended in excess of twenty of them. They were international: Eqypt, a river boat on the Danube river, and a train trip in Mexico along Copper Canyon.

My hobbies are pencil drawing of interesting faces and also writing poetry, and wood carving.

We sold our house in Tulsa and moved to Silver Arrow Estates in 2016.

I have no religious affiliation, finding it difficult to accept some of the edicts presented. I am not an atheist, but probably an agnostic. I simply do not know, but I don't deny those who feel they do.

Nate Clark August 2, 2022

Willie Jean Coats

My Brief History.

I was born on February 8, 1927, in that little town of Scipio, Oklahoma. I grew up with six sisters and three brothers. Ten kids growing up in that small town. My parents told me that I was named Willie after my grandfather, William, who had passed two years before I was born. I went to a one-room schoolhouse in the countryside of Salina for the first four grades. We knew we were poor, but nobody told us. At the age of six, a teacher gave me a little wax doll. Oh, the toys back then were so different. And then high school in town, remembering when I would swing on a rope at the swimming hole. When the pond froze over, we'd go skating.

After graduating, my oldest sister's family and I moved to Seattle, Washington.

I'll always remember that day of Dec 7, 1941, when Pearl Harbor was bombed. During the second world war, we ladies, known as "Rosie the Riviters." worked in factories on the Boeing B-29 airplane.

When the war ended in '45, and the soldiers returned, we had to find other work to support ourselves. During the war, I had been sending and receiving letters from a boy named Howard, whom I met in the fifth grade. He was in the Navy. When he returned, we got married and stayed with it for 68 years.

One of the happiest days, was when my son was born, and I named him Kendal. Howard got a good job in Pryor as a maintenance supervisor for the city.

Knowing this, Philippians 4:18: "I can do all things through Christ who strengthens me" guided me throughout our marriage and life.

I was proud of having taught myself bookkeeping, and I got a job as a State Farm Insurance Agent for thirty-three years. My first car was a 1940 Chevrolet.

Someone asked me, 'if my life was a movie, who would play you?' "Goldie Hawn," I replied," because she's spunky like me."

A special memory is of the time when Howard and I took our great-granddaughter, Britani, three-years-old then, swimming, fishing, picnicking, and to Blue Grass festivals along with country-western singing. She saw papas orange cap that he wore while deer hunting hanging on a rack, along with binoculars, and she said, "let's go bird hunting."

Howard retired in 1962, so we got a fifth-wheel camper and did some traveling to Blue Grass Festivals in Arkansas, Mourissori, and Oklahoma. Did that and more for thirteen years. We never did go to Europe or anywhere overseas as I did not want our money to go there, when it is needed here in America. After retirement I took dancing lessons, and started dancing with a couple around Wagoner, Chelsea, and Muskogee at Senior Citizen dancing events.

My husband Howard had a stroke on our 68th anniversary, December 6, 2015. He passed on the twentieth.

Well, here I am at an independent Living Home in Broken Arrow, Silver Arrow Estates, now named Morada, moving here on July 15, 2016. It is a good place to be.

After a fall, I had total knee and hip surgery along with a broken foot. Time in the hospital and then re-hab.

I had the most wonderful surprise last month when a niece and her husband from Hanah, OK. came to see me. They were here about thirty minutes, and someone knocked on the door, and in walked a niece and her husband from Phoenix, Az, and another niece from Denton, Tx. Oh, what a wonderful surprise. We had such a good day. What fond memories.

Now to all who may read this, may God bless you abundantly as He has to me.

I will remain here, the Lord willing, until He calls me home. I would like to be remembered as a good Christian wife, mother, and grandmother.

Priscilla Ann (Cookie) Jones Collins

I was born on August 23, 1942, in East Chicago, Indiana. I was named Priscilla Ann Jones. My dad gave me the nickname Cookie after Dogwood and Blondes new born baby girl. He always read and enjoyed reading the cartoons to us from the Sunday papers. The nickname carried with me the rest of my life. My three brothers and one sister, and my mom all called me Cookie and still would if they were alive.

I graduated Kindergarten in Hammond, Indiana in 1947. We lived in Hammond until I was six years old. Sadly, my father left the family in the middle of the night after coming home from a night of drinking and was very violent with the family. He left a note telling mom not to come looking for him as we were better off without him, and we surely were as long as he drank. Needless to say, I still loved my dad and missed him very much, as he was gentle and kind when sober!

We moved in with an aunt and uncle in southern Illinois, where my mother grew up, and at eight years old, we moved to Albion, Ill, and started grade school in third grade. I lived there the rest of my growing up years. I was a very sad girl growing up. I went to Albion Grade School and graduated eighth grade, and then started High School. I quit school my sophomore year as I needed to go to work. I worked the rest of my life until I retired at sixty-five years of age. I did not ever like Albion as a young girl.

My mother saw that we came to know who Jesus was, and at eleven years old, I went to the altar and asked Jesus into my heart. Although I didn't understand the things of God, I knew I needed Him and that He loved me. I trusted Him, and for me, that was a big thing. Our mother saw that all five of her children were in church every Sunday. I know now how her prayers and the prayers of those people in the church have kept me all of my life. Today, I am very thankful and humbled.

When I entered the teen years, I started drifting away from my church, and as it goes, many wrong choices were made, but just like my mom, God still loved me and carried me. He says, "I will never leave you or forsake you," and He never has!

As I said earlier, I never liked living in my home-town, so at nineteen, I bought a one-way ticket to Chicago as I had a friend that let me live there with them until I could get a job and my own place to live. I worked in Chicago for a while and then went back home. I worked at many different jobs and in many different towns.

I remained single until I married the first time when I was twenty-six. We were married three-years and a baby boy was born on November 13, 1971. A beautiful child we named Kip. Sadly on December 1, 1971 his biological father was killed in a car wreck. My baby was about three-weeks old. I was very angry with God as I never wanted to raise my child without his father. I made a lot of bad choices because I was angry. Again, I say that God carried me through my grief and anger as He knew the sincerity of that little girl's heart when she asked Jesus into her heart at eleven years old.

When my son was about five months old, I started dating a man and fell in love, and he with me. I married Dick Collins in August 1976, and he adopted Kip and raised him as his own. A wonderful father and husband he was. We were married together forty-five years.

In the meantime, Dick, at age fifty-four, was diagnosed with kidney disease, and his sister donated him a kidney which lasted fifteen-years. Our son had married a girl from Broken Arrow Ok. And he and his wife, along with two boys settled in Broken Arrow. Dick's health was steadily getting worse, and so he moved us to Oklahoma to be close to our son's family. I know now that his time on earth was not to be long. Dick passed away on August 1, 2017. The time of grief was hard, not just for me, but for Kip, Kelly, and two young grandsons who adored their grandfather.

So, here I am again, a widow but this time was different as early in our marriage we came back to the Lord and Savior, and things were easier as I was not mad at God. Oh, grief was hard, and still there five years later, but I know who holds my hand.

Almost three years ago, we sold my house and at eighty years old, I was now living in a retirement facility. God is true to His word, when He says: "I will never leave you nor forsake you," and I have lived to know it.

So much more I could say about what God has done for me, but it would take too long. He said in His Holy Word: "I will make beauty from ashes," and He most certainly did for this girl!

He made something beautiful out of my life.

Sandra Louise Judson David (Sandy)

I was born in 1944 to Ruth and Edward Judson of Danby, New York, a small town nine miles outside Ithaca. My relatives were of German and English descent.

I grew up in a farm house, which had been in the family since 1818 and where my father was born. My brother Steve, twenty months older is now deceased.

Living in the country, playmates were some distance away, so Steve and I entertained ourselves with dress-up games such as cowboys and Indians. Our playground was nine acres of land containing apple orchards and wildberry bushes. In the winter, we patiently waited for Judson Pond to freeze over so we could skate.

When it came time to go to school, we spent grades one to six in a small six-room schoolhouse in the farming community of Danby. I remember visiting a friend after school for a play date, and we would ride her horses. Other activities were church-connected. My family was at the small country church every time the doors were open, as my dad played the organ there for twenty-five years.

For Junior high and high school, we were transported by bus to Ithaca, home of Ithaca College and Cornell University. My mother went back to teaching when Steve and I entered Jr. High, and my father worked in the city as paymaster for the National Cash Register Company. Some of the special memories of going to school in the 'big city' were the football games. My brother played trombone in the marching band, and I was in the Pep Club. When the high school won a game, the band led a pep rally from the school by Cayuga lake up the main street to downtown Ithaca. Other events open to us and our friends as part of a college town were the roller and ice skating rinks on the campuses.

One of the reasons why mom went back to teaching was to save enough money to purchase a summer cottage on Keuka lake, one of the finger lakes of New York State. What a super incentive for my brother and I, to work hard and pass all our courses, so we could spend summers at the lake! There were dozens of kids on our lake road, and we spent the summers swimming, water skiing, sailing, and sunning with our friends. No one wanted to stay home, go to summer school and only come to the lake with dad on weekends.

Senior High came along, and it was time to get serious about what I wanted to do with my life. Nurturing service-oriented jobs had always interested me. My grandma and aunt had come to live with us after grandmas health started to decline. I saw how much caregiving meant to the person on the receiving end firsthand. In the '60s, girls were getting into teaching or nursing. I decided nursing was the career for me. After graduating in '62, four other girls and I in our senior class went to Genesee Hospital School of Nursing in Rochester, NY.

After two years of study and practical experience, we were allowed to work as Licensed Practical Nurses and earn some money. While finishing our final year qualifying us as registered nurses, my first job was in medical surgical nursing in the hospital where I trained.

During my years in nursing school. I met my first husband, who was working at Genesee as a surgical technician. We dated and married after graduation. Our marriage lasted for twenty-one years and gave us two beautiful daughters, but unfortunately, the marriage ended because we were unequally yoked.

My second marriage was to a singer/entertainer, eighteen years my senior. He had been part of Big Band entertainment in his early years but was now retired. We were free to travel and entertain according to our schedule. We spent much of our time traveling to see the kids and grandkids. On the way, we would entertain at independent retirement facilities, such as Morada, delighting seniors with the songs they know and love from the Big Band area. People assumed because he had a wonderful voice, that I could also sing. They could not have been more wrong! I was his "roadie," booking his performances, driving to venues, and running his music while he entertained. He passed away in 2015 due to complications from Parkinson's disease. Our almost twenty-six years of marriage worked because we were equally yoked-me, a believer in Christ since my childhood, and Jay was a Jewish believer since his early twenties, years before we met.

Over the years, I have been blessed to be part of many loving and supportive church families. My faith has brought me through many challenging and turbulent times.

- Divorce after twenty-one years of marriage to my children's father.
- Radiation, chemo, and surgery for cancer in 2006
- Loss of my mom, dad, and brother.
- Loss of my second husband in July 2015.
- My oldest daughter's diagnosis of a brain tumor in Sept 2015.

God is good!

After two surgeries, radiation, chemo, and speech therapy, Michelle continues to have clear MRIs, and I am very hopeful for her future.

Four years ago this past August, I moved to Silver Arrow Estates, now Morada, to be near my youngest daughter Amy's family and to see four of seven of my grandchildren grow up. Again, the Lord blessed me by completing my relocation near family before the pandemic.

I love it here and plan to stay till the Lord moves me to my eternal home.

Jimmy Harlon Ellis

Five minutes after midnight, Sept 4th, 1946, Reba and Harlon Ellis welcomed their firstborn child at 8 lbs, 11 ozs with ten toes, ten fingers, two eyes, two ears, and one nose with two holes already in it.

I don't remember much of the first two years. However, years later, I asked my mother how old was I when you were holding me close to you? I do remember a bottle. (I always thought I was a breast-fed baby).

Anyway, we were sitting in a room, sitting close to a potbellied stove in a rocking chair. For some reason, I was crying. She thought for a minute and said it was right before my sister, Janie, was born. She is a little over two years younger than me.

I was about ten to eleven years old when my uncle Tommy who's two years older than me playing in the harvested corn stubble, playing tag, I think.

Right before I reached the age of going to school, we were in the process of moving from Colorado to Tulsa, we stopped at my dad's folks in Scklirius. Dad had an old chevy car and he had just topped off oil and water plus aired up the tires to same pressure in each tire. One of my uncles, dad's brother Melvin, my aunt, and my cousin were there to see us off. Dad was doing something in the car, and my uncle Melvin walked behind the car to the other side.

Well, I loved my uncle, so I followed. I didn't act like a pest, so I was still behind the car when dad started to move the car. The rear bumper knocked me down. Everybody on the porch saw me walk behind the car and saw me as I went down, and they started screaming. Dad stopped quickly but not quick enough when I fell and rolled with my head in front of the backing-up rear tire. The tire barely touched my head, moving it two or three inches and sliding it across the grass tearing almost both ears off my head.

When they drug me out from the rear of the car, my ear was hanging down, and I think I had a nosebleed.

They wrapped a towel around my head, covering both ears, and went to the hospital doctor. The closest doctor was in a small office where he sewed my ears back up. I remember he gave me a little plastic cup which looked like tomato juice marked with aspirin, I think. I know I was feeling no pain. The doctor said to mom and dad to thank the Lord because had the tire been a little deflated, the tire would have crawled over my head instead of just pushing it.

We made it to Tulsa and on our new adventure. Shortly after the move, my sister Janie was born. Dad went back to work at some lawn care company. By then, winter was on when dad said he'd pick up the limbs the guy had cut if they were thin enough. Dad would put them thru the wood chipper. They had a 55-gallon barrel with the lid cut off. They were burning wood to stay warm.

Dad was still looking for any other kind of work. He had put his application to Douglas Aircraft. They called, and he went to work quickly.

Several years and several moves later, we moved out west to Berry Hill community. From there, we would drive into Tulsa to go to church. Almost immediately, dad felt the Lord calling him into the ministry. He was still working at Douglas, so he started studying by correspondence to become a minister in the Church of Nazarene denomination. After completing his studies, dad got his first church in Skiatook, Oklahoma.

We were in several churches growing up, sometimes for two to seven years. I learned early on I wouldn't get close friends. Sometimes we'd change churches in the middle of the school year. I hated to come into a class after it had been going a while.

I grew up and graduated from high school, and joined the Navy in 1966. One guy from school joined the National Guard or the Reserves. Another guy, however, joined the Navy. I saw him in uniform, and I really liked to dress in bell-bottom pants.

Right after boot camp, I went to become a radio man. The Navy sent me to school to learn morse code and how to manage several radio receivers. I had to take a course in electronics at Class A school.

My first duty station was in Adak, Alaska, on the Aleutian Island toward Russia. The island was nine by fifteen miles, with an elevation of three feet. It was called the birthplace of the winds. Going to the radio station, the rain or snow would be blowing straight across the road, as seen through the windshield going left to right over us. I was there in Adak for twelve months. I filled out my dream sheet requesting my next assignment be in the Philippines. Warmer climate.

They sent me to Vietnam. My intention was to stay in the Navy and retire at Thirty-nine years old.

Vietnam changed that. We were trained one way, and when we got to Nam, we were told to forget all we were taught and do it another way.

Then, after all the riots and protests over the Vietnam war (ah, skirmish), our governments way of explaining it, Nixon started downplaying the importance of our even being in Vietnam and limited us on what we could or could not do.

After almost a year of changes, I had enough. The officers were always on my boat, River Assault Squadron CCB 151-1, a command Communications Boat where all the big-shot commanders were. After one bloody fight, I asked one of the commanders how I could leave Vietnam and the service. He said the only legal way was to extend my duty for six months, and then the Navy would give me a six-month early exit. As soon as I could, that's what I did. By then, I was a second-class petty officer with eleven radios as my responsibility. We had one converted "mike boats." They had two feet of styrofoam with bar armor on the outside. The boats would do about fifteen knots, which was very slow. But we did have a bunch of guns to fire. We were pretty well protected because of the officers on our boat. We traveled with as many as 35 – 40 vessels.

I started writing to a girl while in Vetnam. She was a friend of my cousin. About 6 months later, we were steadily communicating, and I really believe I fell in love with her.

When my time was up. I stopped in Tulsa and had my first date with Dianna.

I had three to four days before I finished my last sixty-two days before discharge. On our third date, I told Dianna, I loved her, she would love me, and we'd get married. That was October, and we got married in March. We have three sons and three daughters-in-law, three grandsons. One died four days before his fourth birthday, five granddaughters but no great grand kids yet.

I studied accounting at OSU Tech in Okmulgee. Stayed there an entire year but never did learn how to program computers. I dropped out and started working with my father-in-law as a sheetrock finisher. After six or seven months, I told him I wanted to be on my own. I learned very quickly, I didn't know it all. However, I really did like the independence of working on my own, so I learned everything I could. I started in Tulsa, but when work slowed, we moved to Texas for a few years. When work in Texas slowed down, we moved back to Tulsa.

My brother-in-law was a finisher also and had moved to Atlanta, Georgia. So, as soon as we could, we moved to Georgia. We were there for three or four years taking on several construction jobs. In De Kalb, just outside Atlanta, we helped start a church with only seven people. Bought some property once owned by Billy Graham, and the church now has over one hundred.

As they were pouring the concrete for the foundation, we all wrapped our Bibles to be waterproof and placed them in the foundation of our new church.

I really miss that Bible, but proud of where it is.

In the middle of 2000, I was diagnosed with kidney damage. And had surgery to remove prostrate and some tumors. Six months later, the cancer retuned. Then chemo and all kinds of drugs. My cancer was not treatable, so doctors could not radiate it. Later in 2000, the doctor told my wife that he has seen others with my condition live for six years or more.

Praise the Lord, I have passed that estimate. I'm 76 today and very glad to be alive and here at this complex with all the nicest people in the world.

I thank God for getting me here.

Arthur Fabrizius (Art)

I was born in Wakeeney, Kansas, on November 17, 1929. My parents were Germans from Russia who came to America at the age of four. German was the first language for all the children in the family. I had two older brothers, three sisters, a younger sister, and three brothers. Ten of us kids.

By today's standards, our life on the farm would have to be considered rather primitive. We had no electricity, no hot and cold running water. Water was warmer in summer and colder in winter, although, I should add, we had to run to get it. Growing up on the farm, we experienced farming the old-fashioned way. Cattle for milk and beef. Chickens for eggs and meat. Hogs for pork meat, along with extensive gardening to help put food on the table, plus canning or storing for the winter months. Farm implements were somewhat modern, although we still had a team of workhorses.

My parents learned English, and we kids learned enough to get by quite well when we started first grade in a rural one-room school in Trego County, Kansas. Our farm was about two and a half miles from the schoolhouse. Many times we walked, weather permitting. Our school had a barn for horses, and some of us got to school on a buggy or rode a horse.

After completing the eighth grade, I attended the town's high school. Graduated and attended Emporia State College, graduating with a bachelor of science degree.

In August 1951, I married my college sweetheart, Loretta Angell. We were blessed with four children, two boys, and two girls. The two boys earned a Ph.D. The oldest is a pastor in the Luthern church and retired in August. The youngest son is a research scientist in the Pioneer division of Dow Chemical. Our youngest daughter is a CPA. Our oldest daughter is a Dental Hygienist.

We were married for sixty-two and a half years when Loretta died in 2014.

My working career for thirty-five years was with a newspaper radio group of eleven newspapers and six radio stations. From a little newspaper in Ottawa, Kansas, the group eventually expanded to eleven newspapers in Kansas, Iowa, and California. The six radio stations were in Kansas, Iowa, Texas, Colorado, and Nebraska.

In January 1935, I was drafted into the U.S. Army. Had basic training in Camp Breckenridge, Kentucky. Then, ordered to report to Ft. Lewis Washington. From there, we sailed on a troop ship to Yokohama, Japan. And from there by rail to Camp Sasebo, Japan, where we were assigned weapons, and sailed for

Pusan, Korea in very early July 1953. There I was assigned to the 24th Reconnaissance Company, 24th Infantry Division, and quartered in a rather primitive POW camp.

The truce was signed after a week or two. After arriving in Pusan, Korea, I was a foot soldier, and my assigned weapon was a Browning automatic rifle. After about two months, I was selected to be the company clerk of the 24th Recon Co. In early January 1954. The division was relocated to an area approximately forty-five miles northeast of Chunchon, putting us much closer to the DMZ. During my tour of duty in the north, I was eventually promoted to Sergeant. My office space was in a Quonset hut which housed the company commander, the 1st Lieutenant, and the warrant officer.

In November 1954, I was rotated back to the States and received an honorable discharge.

In 1997, our youngest son was working in Australia, so we vacationed there for a couple of weeks and also got to see some of New Zealand.

In January of 2002, my wife and I moved from Hutchinson, Kansas, to Broken Arrow. After my wife died in 2014, I continued living in our BA home. Then in July of 2022, I moved to Silver Arrow Estates, now Morada.

J.T. Floyd, Jr

I was born on December 16. 1934 in Shreveport, Louisiana. My parents were from Arkansas and had moved to Shreveport in the late '20s. One sister born in 1936.

Grammar school in Allendale through the fourth grade, and about that time, my father returned from working on the coasts installing guns during World War II. When he returned, we moved to the farm, and I had to change schools to Jewella for 5th thru 7th grade. At the time, there were no middle schools.

Then Fair Park High School for 8th thru 12th grade, from which I graduated in 1953. While there, I had three years of ROTC, and that's when I got my interest in the military. I participated in drill teams and color bearers.

I had several jobs from high school until May of 1954, when I joined the US Air Force, because I was notified that I could be drafted and decided that would be the best choice. This was the beginning of my military career, thinking it would only be for four years.

My first assignment was to Lackland AFB in San Antonio for three months of basic training. I was notified I would be sent to Asia, so I volunteered for Germany. The next thing I knew, I was indeed assigned to Germany. So, in February 1955, I got to ride a ship to a northern German port and a train ride down to Frankfort. There I was assigned a desk job with the Office of Special Investigation. After just a couple of months in the Rhein-Main area, I was sent to Udine, Italy, to do the same job. On my way there, I spent two weeks training in Naples, where I was able to see lots of Rome and Naples. After several months at Udine, the unit was reassigned to Aviano, Italy, and stayed there for only two months. Now it was time for them to send me back to Rhein-Main.

While there, I did a lot of traveling to see several nearby countries. At the end of 1957, it was close to the end of my four-year active duty, and was returned to the states and back to civilian life.

It was now 1958 and time to find a job and ready to settle down. I met up with my ole buddy from the Air Force, and we decided to go to college. After researching several, we decided on Northwestern State College in Natchitoches, La. Since there would be no out-of-state fees and were able to go to college on the GI Bill, Northwestern was our choice.

I majored in Industrial Arts and there met my future wife in an Algebra II class. We got married on May 13, 1960. Then graduation in 1961, and time to look for a job.

As it turned out, I met an Air Force recruiter in the student center, and he convinced me to go back into the AirForce and get a commission, go to pilot school and become a pilot. Sounded very easy. A date was set for the exam for Officer School. On the first day, approximately 40-50 arrived to take it. Only about twenty passed to continue to the second day. Another exam, and about ten passed it to get to go to Officer school, and three to meet a board, that would determine if any qualified to go to pilot school. Somehow I passed and was notified that I qualified for an application to attend the pilot school.

It is now May 1961, and my first daughter is born. And I have been selected to attend Officers School.

In August, I got my commission and assigned to Webb AFB in Big Springs, Texas. I get to fly the T-37 trainer the first six months and then the T-38 for the next six months.

Next assignment was to Hill AFB in Ogden, Utah, and now a co-pilot in the C-124 aircraft. My four years at Hill consisted of my promotion to 1st Lt. Captain. First Pilot. Command Pilot. My tour at Hill consisted of flying to numerous military bases in the US, several islands in the Pacific consisting of Iwo Jima, Wake, Midway, Guam, Johnson Atoll, and countries in Europe. Most flights ended up in Vietnam hauling cargo and troops.

Our second and third girl was born during those years.

My next assignment was a remote tour at Mactan AF in the Philippines for thirteen months. This remote tour was without my wife and daughters. Also, I was not required to fly an aircraft. While at Mactan, I was sent to someplace in Vietnam, which was only a mile away from the northern border. One day a loud explosion went off, and I went over the fence to see what happened. I looked, and all the military folks were running for cover. As it turned out, it was an accident caused by our own troops.

Was I ever made fun of after that.

Back to Mactan to finish my tour and get my next assignment to Seymour Johnson AFB at Goldsboro, NC. Stop off at Merced, California, for training in the KC-135 Tanker. Finally arrived in North Carolina in'68, and again, I fly to numerous bases in the US, the Pacific, Asia, and Europe. Got to pilot the tanker and refuel aircraft, including the Thunder Birds and Blue Angels.

Now it's time for retirement, and it is at SAC Headquarters Offutt AFB in Omaha, Nebraska.

For the next six years, I had a desk job learning how to write programs for computers to process war games. I was still flying but only within the US and Canada. After those six years and twenty years in the Air Force, it was time to retire.

We moved to Dallas, Tx, and I was still writing programs while working for several companies until I got it, it's time to retire again.

We lived in Dallas, four to five years before moving to Broken Arrow, Ok. and then to senior living.

Don Foshee.

I was born on April 8, 1927, in Paris, Arkansas.

I have three sisters, Reba, Ermalee, and Ila Ruth. Brothers Alfred, Doyle, Hubert, and Jackie. I've never had a nickname because what could one do with the name of Don.

In the town of Paris Elementary school, I enjoyed history and Math. In the auditorium, a boy named Charlie threw a piece of plastic that fell off the ceiling at me. I threw it back at him, and I got caught. The principal took me to the office and said, "bend over" for the three or four hits. Charlie did not get punished.

I quit high school in the ninth grade to get work. My first job was in a movie theater, walking up and down the aisle selling sacks of popcorn for a nickel. I charged them fifteen cents for a child and twenty-five cents for an adult. My next job was working at a coal mine, but not underground.

At sixteen, I hitchhiked to California and got a job in a shipyard.

Then, I enlisted in the Navy in 1944. Boot camp in San Diego learning ship service as 3rd Class Peti Officer

Laundryman. I was sent to Hawaii. I spent three years in the Navy.

After service, I married Loreny in September 1947, who I met while working in the theater. Our marriage lasted for fifty years. We had three girls and one boy who went to Tulsa University. The girls took classes at OU to get degrees in nursing to become RNs.

After my time in the Navy, I went back to the coal mine. A brother-in-law asked me to come to Tulsa as a laundry truck driver. Then to Crescent Machanic as trainee #8 to learn to become a machinist with Midwest Instrument, making explosives that the oil companies used to find where oil might be deep underground. I stayed there until I was laid off from Crescent.

Next was with Seargent Brother of Air Craft parts for one year. Stockley called me to work as a supervisor to get back to Crescent.

Most of our vacations were time visiting and helping the family.

I retired in 1994.

I became a member of the Assembly of God Church here in Broken Arrow. My wife died on February 25, 2022, of cancer. We had been in Silver Arrow Estates/Morada about a week before she died.

Anna Lou Goodman

I was born as Anna Lou Warren on February 12, 1931, In Leon, Iowa. I have one sister, Donella, and one brother, Danny.

I fondly remember my kindergarten teacher, Miss Terrasa Tullis, who was very special and kind. We moved to the country after two years to a small farm and a one-room schoolhouse for the first eight grades. About fifteen students there. We loved horse riding, on a wonderful pony named Trixie. We grew produce and popcorn in our garden. We carried water to chickens. We had cattle, horses, and a horned cow named Blackie for milking, plus chickens, one dog and 3 cats.

One day when I was wearing a red dress, the cow picked me up with her horns and tossed me several feet. I wasn't hurt but a very surprised three-year-old.

High School in Leon. My favorite subjects were algebra, Home Ec, a speech class where I had to make a report on a famous woman. Can't remember her name. I was also in the chorus.

I graduated in 1949 and married soon after to a guy who was a student in that small school. He went to work for Great Lakes Pipe Line, and I worked at Rexal Drugs. We had a friend living in Torrington, Wyoming, who encouraged us to move there. Very cold, cold winter. There, my husband worked for JC Penny. We spent about one year there and moved back to Iowa, and he went back to work for the Pipe Line, and I worked in a department store. When a job opened in Barnsdall, Oklahoma, we moved to Tulsa, where I worked in Tulsa school administration. Husband worked in downtown Tulsa for Williams Pipe Line for five years.

On the icy roads in 1977, my husband was fatally injured in an accident. We had two daughters then in college.

Later in 1978, I married Ralph Goodman, who worked for American Air Lines.

When he retired, we bought a Fifth Wheel camper for fishing at Tenkiller lake in April and October and to Rio Grande Valley, Texas in the winter.

As children, we were involved with the Church of Christ. Later we joined the Southern Baptist Church in Tulsa, OK.

Ralph passed away in 2001 after a long battle with Alzheimer's. I continued living in our home in Tulsa until November of 2021, when I moved to Silver Arrow Estates, now my permanent home.

Ron Allen Grossman

I was born in California. Graduated high school in 1962. In high school, I was involved in drama events such as Romeo and Juliet. The West Side Story and others. I had a part-time job at a service station, pumping gas, washing the windshield, and checking tire pressure while the driver sat in the car. In high school, I was on the swim team and also did some wrestling. When applying to college, I wanted to further my involvement in drama, but they told me I was not good enough. My uncle, Pad Richard, was the first person to shoot Marshal Dillion in the TV series "Gunsmoke." My uncle played in many of the western movies back then. So, I was drawn to drama also.

In college, I studied speech therapy to improve my skills. That was 1966. I got a bachelor's degree in Speech therapy. I then got a master's degree in Education in 1972.

I was a cheerleader in college sports events. Three of us guys and a girl would ride around the stadium in a VW, yelling and encouraging the crowd.

I have a sister who lives in Washington State, 13 years younger, but no brothers.

I never served in the military. Was not called up for the draft as I was exempt because of my education degrees.

I met Barbara in Sept. 1967 and married her in August 1968. We had met in a speech therapy meeting.

After college graduation, I worked for a company doing speech therapy and later opened my own practice, attracting clients who felt they needed some therapy. I contracted with Hospitals to refer patients who would benefit from speech therapy to me. I did that for 29 years. I had to have a phone in the bedroom, as I would often get a call late at night, like three in the morning, and have to get to a hospital right then.

My speech therapy practice included children and adults who presented issues with swallowing disorders, stroke, and head injury patients, voice disorders, reduction of foreign accents, delayed articulation, and language disorders. I lectured at two medical schools and a dental school. They kept asking me back, so they must have liked the presentations.

Oh, travels. Barbara and I have been to every continent and every country except Germany and Russia. We've taken many cruises, which last from 21 to 30 some days. In the Philippines, we were walking along a street when a local boy ran up to me and grabbed my shirt sleeve, saying, "Hi, American." His mother took him away, and he said, "bye American."

In S. Africa, a mother invited us into her home with a fenced-in backyard. Very nice. Her three-year-old girl asked me for some money. I gave her a twenty-dollar bill, and she ran off with it. Her mother took it away and handed it back to me, and I later gave it back to the girl.

Oh, I discovered that local people all over the world are very nice, and just wonderful to talk with. So interesting.

In Rome, Italy, the tour guide took us into the back of the Vatican. Three priests, looking like they were armed under their robes, came out, one going to our right, the other to our left, and the last straight away from us. Then more priests appeared, followed by the Pope. He walked past us, an arms-length away. His eyes were always straight ahead. I waved at him, but he did not wave back.

We got to France and stood before the Eifel tower. On a ship to Norway, we renewed our marriage vows. I think S. Africa was my favorite country to visit.

On a cruise trip to South America, at the time of the Covid pandemic 2019, we were quarantined to our cabin for two and a half weeks. A big ship with about 800 passengers. Imagine that, being locked up in close quarters for that length of time. The ship made its way to the Panama Canal but was not allowed to enter. The chief officer announced that at least eight folks had died of the flu.

We cruise a lot, allowing us to meet people from all over the world. We have kept in contact with some of them for many years. In Israel, we hired a private guide, and when we met him, he told us that he had a doctorate degree in archeology, and we got a behind-the-scenes tour.

I retired in 2006, moved to Tulsa, and back to California, following my grandkids and daughter. Finally, back to Broken Arrow, and here we are in Morada in March of 2021.

Cheryl (Cheri) Yvette Jackson.

Welcome to a Snippet of my life!

I was born July 9, 1951, in Searcy, Arkansas. At the time, we were living with my grandmother while Dad was in Korea, serving his country as a medic for the U.S. Army. Thirteen months later, when my Dad came home, we finally met! And yes, I was a Daddy's girl! Upon his return, we eventually moved to Fort Sill in Lawton, Oklahoma, where I was raised, along with my older sister. Dad was ranked as a Staff Sargent and worked at the clinic on base. He served his country for 20 years. He was my hero because he had a great work ethic and was a great family man.

Favorite childhood memory? When the family would visit my grandparents in Arkansas!

A news event you recall growing up? The Vietnam War. It was on television every night.

I was a bookworm, and my best subject in school was English. I also dreamed about becoming a doctor but didn't see it through.

At the age of 18, 1969, After I graduated from Eisenhower High School, I soon married, had two daughters, Wendi and Amber. I got my first job as the secretary for the base Colonel at Ft. Sill.

Five years later, in 1974, I began my career with the US Army Corps of Engineers as a Program Analyst, which is where I met my husband, Jimmy, who was an Electrical Engineer. It was a love that grew stronger each day! We had 24 wonderful years together, and now I'm blessed with the love of four grandchildren and three great-grandchildren! My girl's teacher once told me I was a great Mom, which was the best compliment I ever received. Being a Mom and coaching soccer when my girls were young was the happiest time of my life,

Riding a motorcycle was the craziest thing I ever did. My first car was a 1964 VW Beetle ... stick shift.

Jimmy and I had a great adventurous time when we went on a three-week excursion to Germany, Italy & more!

I've been asked, If I was a warning label, what would you say? No Smoking!

Today I read at least three books a week!

Slow down, folks, to have and enjoy a successful life with the love of your family and talking to your children, and be kind to one another!

My favorite Bible verse is John 3:16

Jeanette James

This is my story. I was born August 16, 1954 in Tulsa, Ok. We lived at that time on 54th st. in North Tulsa. Mom was of German Irish descent, but Dad never talked about his. Mom passed at the age of 92, and my Dad, who had diabetes, had a stroke on New Year's Eve and passed on New Year's day at the age of sixty-eight. I have one brother and one sister.

Elementary school was at Alcott, but nothing special there.

Junior High for two years at Gilcrease. High school at McLain. I was in the choir and also helped put together backgrounds_for drama presentations. I_wanted to go to California, so Dad and Mom took me there for six months staying in Pamona, where I attended high school. Those were the days of numerous civil riots tearing parts of California apart. Two boys started to fight outside our school. Another group was putting single-edge razors in the girls hair, so when the girls reached up to remove the razor, blood would be on her hands. Oh, I just went to the classes and quickly went home.

We moved back to Tulsa and back to McLain high school. I met my first husband there, and I married him at the age of seventeen. Had one daughter on January 28, 1974.

Divorced at twenty-one. Then two more marriages, which I won't discuss those. After all that, I met and married Bill James, which lasted for twenty-two years. He worked for GC Broma, installing heaters and exchange units. Bill had a stroke and passed.

My first job was when I was living with my grandmother. I started in the café of a motel in Carthage, and several jobs after that, including a Texaco convenience store, and ended up working at Braum's for five years.

I now have four grandchildren and six great-grandchildren.

I Lived in Coweta and attended the Baptist Church for eleven years. At the age of forty-three, I had a stroke. I thought I had gone blind, but God was there and brought me through all that.

I then lived with my granddaughter for a year. Then to Prairie Rose Senior living, and not satisfied with that place, I finally moved here to Silver Arrow Estates/Morada four years ago.

The first couple of years here, I was bitter and angry about everything.

But God has changed me. I looked up to God and I heard: "it is finished." Everything before that point is done and over with. That part is finished.

I wear a smile, have become friendly, enjoying the life here at Morada.

It is finished.

Hannelore Jiehl.

This will be short, as Hannelore had just a few minutes to talk, as she was moving out of Morada the next day to live with her daughter twenty minutes away from the beach in South Carolina.

I was born on February 9, 1935 in Manheim, Germany. Moved to the US in 1955 to Wewoka, Oklahoma. My husband's hometown. I met him in Germany on one of his tours to Germany as part of the US Army. We had 63 wonderful years together. Growing up in Germany, I wanted to be a ballerina. I loved to dance, but dad said NO. I was also interested in sports and arts. My parents lost everything during the war.

We have one daughter, '56, and two sons '57 and '59. Of his twenty years of service, he had been stationed in Germany for three years, back to the states, and two more transfers of spending three years each in Germany. He was offered a job as an intercom system specialist in Bellingham, Washington moving there in '89.

After he retired, I worked at a local college doing administrative services and assistant Student Services. I went to the University of Tulsa 1981-'85 and got a music and International studies degree.

My two sons joined the US military. One in Navy, the other in Army.

My first car was a 1950s' Mercury.

My husband was diagnosed with Alzheimer's in 2014, and spent time in two nursing homes. We sold the house in 2016, and he passed on April 19, 2017.

Fred Jostes

I was born in Springfield, Ill, on Aug 16, 1937. I had two brothers, one three years older, one 1 ½ years older, and a sister six years younger. My oldest brother passed 25 years ago because of cancer. Dad bought a farm in Rochester, Ill., in 1940 with no plumbing or electricity. In '46, we got plumbing and electricity in 1950.

My great-grandmother had some property in Springfield and gave it to the Methodist Church. They built Asbury Methodist Church and a parsonage there. My mother went to that church before getting married, and that's where she met my dad. We went to that church every Sunday morning and Wednesday night prayer meeting. The church was ten miles from the farm. My family was always strong church attenders. I had three uncles as pastors of churches; a Methodist and two Baptists. I had three cousins that became Methodist pastors.

There was a revival at Asbury in Springfield when I was about ten. At the end of the service, I felt an impulse and went forward to the altar to dedicate my life to Christ. I accepted Jesus as my savior.

When we got older, we went to MYF on Sunday nights. Attended Church camp for four years.

My first school was one room with one teacher for all grades. I attended that school for three years, and when the school was consolidated, I went to Rochester for the remaining years and graduated from high school in 1955. I was active in sports, with baseball as my favorite. I became a St. Louis Cardinals fan. I did not attend college but always loved math, taking every math class because I thought that was the easiest. That helped because it got me into a four-year apprenticeship at Caterpillar Tractor Company. We would work six hours and go to school for two hours.

I got married in 1958. We had four kids. After the third was born, a boy, I decided to convert to Catholicism. We attended church off and on. Not good Christians. We were married for 15 years, then divorced. I had nearly drifted into a very sinful life, no longer attending church. The devil had taken over my life. I was obsessed with bowling, which led me to bad contacts, drinking, and being involved with people of evil influence.

I met Glenda about a year after my divorce, got married in the Luthern church, joined, and we were part-time Christians. We were married for 44 years and had two kids. Glenda had not been raised in a Christian home, and I was trying to straighten up my life at the time.

That was hard. I wanted to get back into a stronger Christian life but failed. I still had habits that were hard to give up. Daily temptations lead me astray. I allowed that to happen, of course,

I took early retirement from Cat after 35 years. Moved to Pryor to work for Pryor Foundry. I felt that God led me to Pryor to get me away from the bad influence that kept me away from church. We started attending St. Johns Lutheran church and became an elder there for four years.

I was approached by my old supervisor from Cat to go to China. I took that position that proved to be very rewarding. There were some of my co-workers in China who were interested in Christianity. I took some bibles with me on the second trip. There was an underground church in the village where I lived. I wanted, but I was told I couldn't because if the party found out, it would be bad for all. I found that General Chiang Kia-Shek was a baptized Methodist. There was a Catholic church near that we were allowed to attend, which I never did. I returned to Pryor and found that the pastor had changed. We did not get along, so I tried the Methodist church. Liked it and became a member.

I did have an interesting experience. I worked in India for three months. The gentleman next to me on my flight home asked if I had gone to Thomas's Mount. I had not and didn't know what he meant. He told me the story that the apostle Thomas had been killed in India. I was not aware of that, so I looked it up on google. Yes, Thomas was in India spreading Christianity and was murdered by a Hindu priest.

My faith increased. Started getting more involved, but not so much as I should have. I did attend almost every Sunday. Glenda started reading 'Jesus Calling' and got more involved and increased her faith, and I feel she accepted the Lord as her savior before she passed two and one-half years ago. I moved to Broken Arrow and went to and joined Asbury Methodist church in Tulsa.

I had been studying the bible, not just reading it, but trying to study and understand the history of the early Christians. Jesus is now part of my everyday life. He gives me peace and is leading me every day. I am now reading the book "Jesus Calling" daily. I would also read three chapters of the old testament and then read three chapters of the new testament.

I know now that Jesus never left me. I left Him. He was always there anytime I needed Him. He watched over and protected me. There are several times in my life that I know He was there keeping me safe.

My dad went to heaven in 1965. My mom was a guiding light for me. She became a housemother at Lincoln Christian College after dad passed. She worked there for 15 years. She was on a prayer team, and I knew she prayed for us kids daily. I saw her and dad's faith and decided I wanted their peace of mind

I know 2020 was a very trying time, but I knew the Lord was there protecting us. It is hard to keep the faith when you don't meet with other Christians on a weekly basis. The way things are in the country now shows that we need the Lord more than ever.

I have attended several different churches; Methodist, Catholic, Baptist, Lutheran, and Assembly of God. One thing that it taught me is that we worship the same Jesus Christ. They just worship in different ways. That doesn't make anyone right or wrong. Just read the scripture and make up your own mind. Everyone can get a different interpretation of what they read. I know I have read different scripture, then went back and thought that isn't what I understood it to say before. Never stop reading scripture and studying the Word of God. Interpretations changes as our faith grows. God will lead us down a path. It is up to us to follow the right path and continue to grow in faith.

Jesus taught the disciples to be aware of false prophets. Be sure you are being taught from scripture, and don't be led down the wrong path. The devil will use all methods to deceive us.

I heard a lesson at a children's church. It says Christians are like a charcoal fire, and when you are in contact, the fire will grow strong. But if you pull a piece away from the group, it will eventually go out. Christian faith is the same way. If the group stays together, the fire will grow. Separate, and it will falter. That is why it is necessary that you meet every week. Online is not the same as personal contact.

Arnold R. Kropp (Arnie)

I was born in August, 1938 in the windy city of Chicago, Ill. I've got three brothers. All of us four years apart,

Oh, I got in trouble in elementary school. The girl screamed, and the teacher came to see. She grabbed my ear and led me to the principal's office to experience the wood trouble solver. I never did that again. It was nothing serious. The girl could just cut an inch off her pigtail that I had dipped in my ink well.

I graduated on time, so high school was next. Drafting was my favorite subject getting A's all four years and winning a few contests with my designs. I'll not mention how I did in the other required subjects, especially Mathematics. One day playing on the baseball team, a hard-hit line drive broke my second finger when I used my hand to catch the ball instead of using the glove. When the inning finished, it was turn to bat. You can imagine what a swollen middle finger looked like holding the bat. Anyway, I was sent to the bench.

My first job was bicycle delivering the Chicago Tribune to homes in the neighborhood, collecting the monthly fees, and keeping my commission. During the Thanksgiving and

Christmas holidays, I sold neckties and shirts in a department store on a commission-only basis.

When eleven of us boy scouts graduated in '56 the scoutmaster took us on a two-week camping canoe trip into beautiful southern Canadian lakes, streams, and yes, some portages to the next lake. Entering one lake, we saw a resort and paddled there. We were treated as royalty. Gave us a hot sauna bath and then told to run out to jump in the lake.

College was next, a small Christian one in southern Wisconsin because I flunked the math test required to pursue a degree in Architecture. The Freshman Dean had a meeting with us and explained he lived next to the dorm and did not want us to throw our beer cans out the window landing in his backyard. Nothing special there. I was part of the golf team.

After three and a half years of studying subjects I had no interest, I dropped out and joined the US Army in January 1960. Sent to Ft. Leonard Wood for basic and then three months at Ft. Knox, where I learned the Morse Code. Then to Schwabach, Germany. I became part of a Long Range Recon Patrol. Oh, we did a lot of walking through the forests of southern Germany during the peaceful cold war years of '60-'62.

On one training trip, we were sneaking down from a ridge to a stream, and then to go up the other side. Half-way down, we heard ping, ping, ping whistling over our heads. We hit the ground. We discovered we were in the middle of a British firing range. Our Sergeant then said he led us there as part of our training. "Thanks Sarg!"

On another day, I was riding along with four other gi's in the back of a truck. The truck swiftly slipped and turned over in the ditch. My left arm was broken half way between the elbow and wrist. Spent a few days at the Army hospital in Frankfurt. The doctor put pins through the marrow of those two bones. Sent back to base in a sling. No cast.

I was fortunate on one leave to visit west Berlin, summer of '61. At the East-West German dividing line a few hours west of Berlin, I had to stop to show my papers. The guard said, "your trip to West Berlin is timed. Do not get off the autobahn." In Berlin, I saw where the Russians were blocking up the Brandenberg Gate and using circular barbed wire on the east/west dividing line of Berlin.

One four-day trip down to beautiful, peaceful Switzerland. I could hear cow-bells across the valley.

On another leave, driving a '49 VW up to and through Denmark to Copenhagen to catch the ferry boat to Malmo. Driving off the ferry into town, I immediately learned to drive on the left side of the street through Malmo, across southern Sweden up to Stockholm. My mother had a cousin living there who took me water skiing behind his Chris Craft Mahagony hull boat on the Baltic Sea in those cold, cold waters. North of his villa, I got to view the magnificent dancing of the Northern Lights. Wow!

I was discharged in December '62, worked a bit in Chicago, then moved to Atlanta, Ga, and returned to college seeking a sociology/psychology major. Ha. Boring.

The next summer, I was part of a student exchange program and assigned to live with a German family and work in his factory for ten weeks. One day, the owner asked me to accompany him on a business trip through Check-Point Charlie into East Berlin. He had a new Mercedes Benz, I think it was. As we sat at an outdoor café, a bunch of East Berlin German folks gathered around looking at his car. A young fellow approached, and they all scattered. The boss told me that guy was an informer.

Back to Atlanta and college, and to work in an auto manufacturing plant to cover expenses. Quit that after thirty days, when I was required to join the union. My arm was still not healed. A doctor then operated on it and removed bone chips from my hip to insert where the bones met. He also removed the pins, and then, the arm was put in a cast.

Then I got job in a city recreation center, where I met my first wife, who had a toddler son from her first husband, then deceased. I quit school, married her, was hired, and trained as a store manager for FW Woolworth. We moved to West Hollywood Florida for training, and I ended up managing a store in Bartow, Fla. several years. Six years with Woolworth.

Then the big box stores emerged, and Woolworth suffered. I was hired to manage a fabric store. I did not know a thing about fabrics and sewing, so, for two-weeks training of feeling different fabrics etc. I helped the company open a new store in Ft. Pierce, Florida. That evening, the company president took me out to dinner. He told me we helped you to get the store opened. It was great. Now, anytime you need help, give us a call, run the store as if it was yours, and at the end of the year, you will get ten percent of the profits.

One day the high school Home Ec. teacher was there with her students. I suggested that the store provide the pattern, the fabric, threads, and buttons to her students, if they would parade their created gown down a thirty-foot-long platform in front of customers on a Saturday. They did and loved it, as the customers did also.

The company was expanding, opening five stores in the suburbs of Chicago, and I was transferred to Aurora, Ill. That lasted a few years as polyester became a big item in the ready-to wear clothing business. It became easier to buy clothes than to sew, and home ec sewing classes diminished. Another company hired me to manage two stores in Grand Rapids and Lansing in Central Michigan.

We now had two more sons, Douglas, Brian, and one daughter Cynthia. I got us a pop-up tent trailer for camping in Northern Michigan. Those were great times.

Then that company went belly up.

A church acquaintance hired me to sell and deliver canned goods, sweet stuff like donuts, and such as Pepperidge Farm Cookies to grocery stores and quick stops in Kalamazoo, Mi.

We had good years in Wyoming, just south of Grand Rapids, even though the area had lots of snow over the winter months blown in from Lake Michigan. Then in 1979 I felt called to Broken Arrow to attend the Rhema Bible School. We moved to Broken Arrow in July. It was 102 the day we arrived, setting up camp in a Catoosa campground, now a shopping center. Why so hot?

I got the two-year Rhema diploma while working nights for Quick Trip, but never felt called into full-time ministry. In 1981, my two oldest sons, then seventeen and fifteen, and I joined a Tulsa Group bicycling from Texas to Kansas in seven days. Brian, then thirteen, could have gone, but I thought fifteen was the youngest allowed for that long trip.

I bought a restaurant on Main St. BA where my wife, a fantastic cook, worked and ran the place for a year and a half as I was working nights for QT. Sales dropped. I closed it and auctioned off everything.

My wife, Louise, and I were having problems and divorced 1987.

I floundered around for a year or so at various jobs. Talked to Wall-Mart about management but was told I'd have to start at the bottom. I even did semi-trucking for three months, until an experience on the streets of NY City.

A church friend arranged a meeting for a lady they knew from Woodward, Ok. We hit it off right away and married in August 1989. On our honeymoon in a cabin in Colorado, she experienced tremendous pain a few days after enjoying the woodsy cabin. Took her to a hospital in Colorado Springs for examination. They wanted to operate right then and there. No!

We caught a flight to Tulsa. In Tulsa, they said she had Multiple Sclerosis. A bit later, a doctor discovered bone fragments hindering nerve function along her lower back. Those were removed, and she was able to function without pain again, but yet somewhat hindered. She still could not return to her secretarial work again to sit at a desk all day.

I was hired as a convenience store manager, first in downtown Tulsa. Did that until my night manager went missing for a day. He said he was robbed and forced to go with them. I believed him, but the company did not. They fired both of us.

Then in 1991, I was hired by the City of Tulsa as part of a golf course maintenance crew. I enrolled in Rogers State College for a two-year associate's degree in agricultural science. I was promoted to assistant golf course maintenance supervisor.

During this time, my wife Joyce volunteered at St. Frances South, where she met and became friends with some wonderful Catholic ladies who met weekly at various homes.

I retired from Tulsa after twelve years 2003. A year or so later, I took a job as a Broken Arrow school bus driver. Oh, try that sometime. I did survive ten years of that, three years as a special needs bus driver. The best of it was getting to know the other drivers and aides. A great bunch of folks safely driving those kids to and from school.

During the summers, we had wonderful times traveling to a few spots. Once to Urbana, Ill., to visit her brother and niece's family. Another time to Southern Minnesota to visit another relative. Joyce was now wheelchair-bound.

Another time to S. Carolina to visit friends, and from there to Richmond, Va visiting my brother, who took us to Washinton DC. Joyce and I took a tour bus to see the Lincoln Memorial. Taking the elevator up, she discovered she had left her purse on the bus. Another tour bus arrived, and I told the driver what happened, and he took us to headquarters, and low and behold, her purse had been turned in. Nothing was missing. Hallelujah!

Over the next few years, Joyce experienced additional problems, Alzheimer's, stability, and ongoing dementia. She was hospitalized for a fall. Treated, and was assigned to a nursing home for rehab. Then to another, and another, and another, lastly, to one in Catoosa, now under hospice care.

During those times of home alone, in the mornings, I would nibble on a banana, sip my coffee while sitting on the deck watching the birds, squirrels, rabbits etc. One morning, I noticed a bunch of ants crawling from one side of the deck to the other, and straight up a seven-foot high vinyl post and then under the vinyl beam to the hummingbird feeder to get that sweet stuff, and then back down to the nest. Wow, how do they do that?

It was through these experiences that, without a doubt, it strengthened my faith, knowing that there is an Almighty God who created those ants and everything else for us to enjoy and use. No longer did I ponder why or how we got here on this planet, along with the scientists' claim of billions of years of atoms, molecules eventually merging into two eyes to see, two ears to hear, a nose with two nostrils to smell, two lips and two layers of teeth to chew, along with two lungs to breathe and exhale, two arms, two legs, and a brain to process, remember, and to imagine. Hmm? Happenstance? No Way!

Yes, there is a Supreme God who created everything, and that spirit is with us every day, every minute, every second never leaving us, who sacrificed His son Jesus taking upon Himself our disobedience sins. Jesus, a real historical figure, crucified, buried and rose to walk again to forgive, save and fill us, disobedient nobodies, with His spirit.

I started writing. Published the first novel in 2005, then a sequel to it. Continually writing and playing golf, along with visits to see Joyce. Then two more novels. A book about school buses, which I gave copies to my fellow bus drivers and aides. These were all self-published as the mainline large publishing houses demanded huge sums to edit and suggest changes for publishing and possibly hit the bookstores, so I declined and discovered the self-publishing route. My books are not available in book stores as they are labeled as Print on Demand.

Several years of that and then the understanding of getting older and not wanting the additional tasks that come with home ownership, I sold the house in early 2022, and moved into this independent living retirement center. It's been great getting to know these residents. The staff is terrific, and it feels like living in my first mansion. The next is a Heavenly Mansion.

Michael and Karen Mason

On a cold, snowy Valentine's Day in 1951, my father drove my mother to Saint Vincent's Hospital, a three-story gothic-looking building perched on the very top of a steep hill overlooking the Arkansas River Valley in Morrilton, Arkansas. Three hours later I arrived screaming and crying as newborns do, the first of two boys that would form this little family.

For the next three years my parents moved several times to different towns in Arkansas and Oklahoma struggling to make a living and realize the American dream. In 1954 my family, now including my younger brother, Richard, moved to Russellville, Arkansas where my father completed a bachelor's degree in education from Arkansas Tech. **Dad** was the first in his family to go to college, a feat that changed the course and expectations for future generations of the Mason clan.

After completing his degree, Dad accepted a job with the Atkins, Arkansas Public Schools where he taught high school history and coached high school football, basketball, and track during the school year, and worked at the Atkins Pickle Plant in the summer. Mom (Lois Nell

Williamson Mason) drove 14 miles each day to work at Sears and Roebuck in Morrilton. My life in Atkins, where I completed grades 1-5, was fun and uneventful. We attended sporting events several evenings a week and on Sundays attended worship at the Atkins Church of Christ. We frequently visited grandparents, aunts, uncles, and cousins in the Morrilton area and I thought life was grand.

Then in the summer after my 5th grade year, my father announced that we were taking a trip six hours north to a town on Lake of the Ozarks called Camdenton, Missouri for a job interview. At that time Arkansas teachers were paid a pittance and if he got the job in Camdenton, his salary would double. After a successful interview, Dad was offered the job and four weeks later we were living in a small, two-bedroom cabin and learning what for me was a new way of talking, interacting, and doing church. I was not a happy camper and made sure my parents knew about it.

In spite of my unhappiness at having my little world turned upside down, I now look back and realize that this move had a big impact on helping me expand my horizons and understand that there was more to this world than the little town and life I had become comfortable with in Atkins. Though I was never a "Missourian" at heart, I did learn a lot and adapted to a new way life - though I never liked the way they laughed at me for speaking "southern" and saying "Yes ma'am and no sir."

In 1969, after graduating from high school, I headed back to Arkansas and attended Harding College in Searcy for four years, earning my degree in elementary education in 1973.

However, my primary accomplishment during those four years was meeting and falling in love with a beautiful young lady from New Egypt, New Jersey, Karen Lynn Lemmons. After a nine-month courtship, Karen and I married in New Jersey on May 27, 1972, at the end of my junior year. We honeymooned at a friend's cabin in Maryland on the Chesapeake Bay. Afterward, we returned to Searcy where we rented a furnished duplex two blocks from the Harding campus where I finished my senior year and Karen, who had already completed her degree in history, worked full-time at the Harding library. At the end of that school year, I graduated and was hired to teach 5th grade for Harding Academy in Memphis, Tennessee.

Karen got a job as receptionist at a branch of the National Bank of Commerce in Memphis.

I loved teaching school and at the end of that first school year Harding asked me to serve as principal at one of their nine elementary schools. Though surprised, I accepted the offer and immediately enrolled at Memphis State University and began working on my Masters in Elementary School Administration and Supervision and completed that degree two years later. I had a wonderful staff of teachers and students and thoroughly enjoyed my three years at that school. Then another big change happened when our first son was born. Todd Anthony Mason rocked our world, and we decided it was time to leave Memphis in order to raise him in a calmer, safer environment. I began looking for another job opportunity.

That spring, Karen and I went to visit some college friends from Harding who lived in Mountain Home, Arkansas. When we arrived, we thought it was about the prettiest little town we had ever seen. In the middle of the Ozark Mountains and surrounded by Lake Norfork, Bull Shoals Lake, the Buffalo National River, and the world-famous White River trout fishing paradise, we fell in love with the place. We shared with our friends that, with the arrival of our first son, we were looking to leave Memphis. The wife, who taught art for the Mountain Home Schools, told us that the elementary principal was retiring after a long, illustrious career and asked me if I would be interested in applying for that position. Boy, was I!

That same Saturday afternoon, our friend called the Mountain Home school superintendent and told him she had a friend in town who was interested in the elementary principal's job. The superintendent told her to have me meet him at his office in two hours. After a nice interview with the superintendent, he picked up the phone and called the retiring school principal and asked her to meet with me at her office that afternoon.

After an interview with the retiring principal and a tour of the school, she then picked up the phone and called the superintendent back and said simply, "Fred, this is the one." *An* hour later I was introduced to the president of the board of education and drove back to Memphis the next day with a new job at double the salary I was making in Memphis. Yay!

Back to my beloved Arkansas in a storybook setting that would prove to be a great season of personal, spiritual, and professional growth. And the crowning glory of those four years was the birth of our second son, Joseph Everett.

Near the end of our fourth year in Mountain Home, Karen and I became a little restless and sensed the Lord's call on us to do some type of mission work, though exactly what and where was still unclear. Then out of the blue a few weeks later, I received a phone call from a man in Fayetteville, Arkansas who introduced himself and told me a friend of his had told him about me and my work. He explained that he and some of his Christian friends in northwest Arkansas were starting a new K-6 Christian Academy in Springdale and he wondered if I would be willing to come talk to them about helping them start the school as their first head master. Karen and I asked each other if this might be the mission to which the Lord was calling us.

We decided to do the interview and after an offer of employment, I accepted the new challenge and we suddenly found ourselves once again packing our bags and moving to Springdale, Arkansas for a new challenge. Before accepting the new job, I shared with the school's board of directors the calling we felt the Lord had put on our hearts to do some type of mission work and that this new school might or might not be the call we were hearing. The board was good with this and so we were in for a great year of Christian education and making new friends.

During Christmas break of that school year, some missionary friends from Lyon, France, that we had known and worked with at Harding, came to visit and spend several days with us in Springdale. We caught up on each other's lives and shared what the Lord had been doing in our lives since we had last seen each other. When Karen and I explained how we had felt the Lord's call on us to go do mission work somewhere they both said that they were really in need of someone to come help them with their church-planting work in Lyon and that they would love for us to consider and pray about raising support to come work with them.

Suddenly things began to come into focus and deep in our hearts, it just felt right. The Lord quickly paved the way for this dream to become a reality and six months later we were unpacking an international shipping container of our most basic possessions and settling into a new life of incredible challenges, adventure, and culture shock in Lyon, France.

In the fall of 1982, Karen and I enrolled in language school at the Faculte Catholique de Lyon, and we enrolled our boys in French public schools. After a few months, our boys were both fluent in French as Karen and I were jealously struggling through adult language school.

Two years later, I completed my degree in French from the University of Lyon and we were busily involved in the work and ministry of the Lyon Eglise du Christ. At the end of our fourth year in Lyon, college friends who were working at a mission in Nantes, France, called and told us they had been invited to teach at Harding for one year as missionaries in residence. They knew that a third couple had announced they were joining our work in Lyon and they asked if Karen and I would consider moving to Nantes to take their place for their year's absence. Karen and I accepted this invitation and for the next five years we threw ourselves into the work and ministry of the Nantes Eglise du Christ.

After nine years of ministry in France, our family returned to Springdale, Arkansas in 1991. I enrolled at the University of Arkansas and acquired a job as elementary principal for the

Pea Ridge Public Schools and Karen was hired as an accountant and office manager for a CPA firm in Fayetteville.

I completed my Specialists Degree in School Administration and Supervision from the U. of A. and worked for five years at Pea Ridge before being hired as principal of Washington Elementary in Fayetteville.

Both sons graduated from high school in Springdale and went on to complete college degrees, Todd at Oklahoma Christian University in Edmond, Oklahoma and Joseph at John Brown University, in Siloam Springs, Arkansas.

In the fall of 2,000, I was privileged to open a brand-new middle school on the west side of Fayetteville. It would prove to be the most difficult, but rewarding challenge of my work career. I worked tirelessly to hire a quality staff and build a school focused on learning and educating students to become productive, ethical citizens who would contribute to the betterment of themselves and their world.

During these years Karen and I also joined with several other families to start a new non-denominational church in Fayetteville, New Heights Church. This new church would prove to be a place of spiritual encouragement and healing for thousands of people from across the religious spectrum, especially those who had been wounded by spiritual legalism.

From its humble beginnings of 55 souls meeting together on its first Sunday, New Heights met an obvious spiritual need and grew to over 2,000 within a few years. To this day it remains a strong force for spiritual reconciliation for many in the northwest Arkansas area. The church hired Karen to be its first secretary and financial accountant in 2005 where she worked until her retirement in 2015. During that time I made an unforgettable mission trip with one of the church's pastors to Mali, Africa. Mali is a French-speaking country, and I translated sermons and conversations between the French and English-speaking people at church and in various small-group meetings.

In 2013, after forty years of work, I retired and we enjoyed living next door to four of our six grandchildren, Anna, Emily, Nora, and Adam, until Joseph and Lindsey moved to Denver to complete their master's degrees at Denver Seminary. When Joseph and his family moved to Denver, Karen and I decided to move to Bixby, Oklahoma to live for a while near our other son and daughter-in-law, Todd and Bekah and enjoy trying to be the best possible Opa and Mimi to our two Oklahoma grandsons, William and Thomas.

And that brings us to the current time where age, health issues, and the concerns and fatigue of home maintenance and repair, caused us to long for a simpler lifestyle (preferably one without shopping, cooking, cleaning, mowing, etc.) So to the computer we went, researching different independent living sites in the Tulsa area. We finally came to visit Carol at Morada in Broken Arrow and after talking with her, touring the building, and meeting many of the friendly folks at Morada, we knew we had found our "mansion".

We have lived in our mansion since October 1, 2022 and have thoroughly enjoyed meeting and making new friends, excellent meals, and a more carefree life style. We think living in our Morada mansion is GRAND! It is the best place we can think of to live until we move one last time, to our mansion above that Jesus is preparing for us. Jesus tells us in John 14, "Let not your heart be troubled: you believe in God, believe also in me. In my Father's house are many mansions. If it were not so, I would have told you. I go to prepare a place for you.

And if I go and prepare a place for you, I will come again, and receive you unto myself; that where I am, there you may be also." PTL!

Michael and Karen Mason

Apartment 204 at Morada, Broken Arrow, OK.

Leona Meadors

I was born on July 19, 1931 as Leona Bowland in McDonald, a western Kansas village near Nebraska.

My dad, Oskar Bowland, of German heritage, moved us to Glen Wood Springs, Colorado, when I was four or five. Dad worked as a carpenter. I was born as the last of five girls and then six brothers, joining us five girls. Eleven of us kids. Mom raised us wonderfully. My grade school was in Silt Colorado, and also high school until I transferred to New Castle, a total of fifty students in the school where I sang in the choir. Our senior class consisted of five girls and one boy. That boy in our class, Herman Dale Meadors ended up as my husband.

I never learned to drive until I was thirty-two, when I had to take driving lessons to get that license.

We had three boys and two girls. Dads brother-in-law took us several times to ride down the Colorado river. It must have been on a raft.

Dale is what I called my husband. He was a teacher of high school mathematics while also coaching some basketball and mostly track teams in three small schools.

I went to college for two years at Greely Co.

Dale was called up for the draft, but he got a deferment for being a high school teacher. During the years of raising the kids, I did a lot of babysitting in our home, and I also worked for a farmer family, who raised corn and wheat. They had four sons helping on the farm. I did lots of weighing of the crops for shipment and storage in the silos. Also handled much of the bookkeeping.

We moved back to Kansas to Garden City, where he taught math at the Community College for twenty years, while also coaching the track team. He worked his way up to the National Director Board of Track and Field. He was awarded to the Hall of Fame in track and Field.

After his retirement, various Kansas schools called on him to be a referee of their track meets.

We always attended the community Presbyterian church in Silt and New Castle. During the holidays of Thanksgiving, we invited twelve boys from the track team over for a big feast. I remember one of those times when two boys were walking behind me. I stopped and authoritatively told them to walk along with me, not behind. We all had a lot of fun during those times, as did the students. It was terrific sharing the feast and having fun times with those kids.

Dale passed in 2010, and my daughter had a small house for me to live here in Tulsa. 2011 is when I moved into Morada, which then was Silver Arrow Estates.

Sue Pahmeier

I was born Katherine Sue Viets, at St. Mary's Hospital in Jefferson City, Mo., on December 2, 1938. I've always been called Sue rather than Katherine. I have one brother Tom, who is two years older. My father died when I was a baby. When I was thirteen, my mother married my step-father, whose wife was deceased, and I got one step-brother and two step-sisters.

From kindergarten through eighth grade, I attended Trinity Luthern School. I loved going to school and was always happy when summer vacation was over, and school started again. My favorite subjects were reading, spelling, history, and geography. The least was math. In the eighth grade, I was determined to be the valedictorian at graduation and worked hard all year, but ended in second place. I was happy about that until I realized I had to make a salutation speech at the beginning of the graduation ceremony.

I graduated from Jefferson City high school in 1956. My favorite subjects were again history and English. In my senior year, I was on the yearbook staff to help organize and select which pictures to use. I sang in the HS choir when I first noticed Bill, who was one grade ahead of me.

Our sports teams were called the Jeff City Jays, and the pep squad was the Jayettes. On game days, we wore our red skirt and black letter sweater uniforms with a red J on it. And, of course, black and white saddle shoes. We sat behind the cheerleaders and cheered with them.

I didn't drive until after Bill and I were married, and he taught me how to use a stick shift car. My stepdad had a car, but it was always in use between him and my two brothers. We had city buses, and I lived close to all the schools, so I could walk or ride anywhere.

I have always wanted to be a teacher. I went to Luthern Junior College in Winfried, Kansas (St. John's College) and got an associate degree with a one-year teaching certificate. I taught second and third grades at St. Luke's Luthern School in Kansas City, Kansas, for two years. I then attended Lincoln University in Jefferson City to update my teaching certificate for another year.

Bill and I met at school. The school was high school juniors and seniors, plus college freshmen and sophomores, all in one building. I was a senior and he was a JC freshman. We knew each other and had talked several times. One Friday night, I went to a drive-in theater with a couple of girls, and he was there with a couple of guys. At intermission, we were both at the snack bar and started talking. He asked if he could take me home and then asked me for a date the next weekend, and not long after that, he asked to go steady.

When Bill graduated, he got a job in Kansas City. I think it had something to do with me being there. We were married on January 1, 1960. Soon after, we moved to Indiana, where our first daughter was born. After three years, we moved to Bartlesville, Oklahoma. Another daughter and a son were born in '63 and '69. Bartlesville was a great town to raise a family. Lived there for thirty years.

When I was young, I traveled with my family to visit relatives in Pennsylvania, Connecticut, New York, and Washington DC. When our children were growing up we took trips to California, the East Coast, and many places in between. Ater bill retired, we traveled all over the country by car to all states except North Dakota and Delaware. Toured seven presidential libraries and seven Civil War Battlefields. Overseas we got to Hawaii, Alaska, Canada, England, Switzerland, Austria, Spain, Portugal, and New Zealand.

After Bill retired, we lived in a development on the Illinois river for four years, then Tulsa for ten years, and Bixby for seventeen years. We moved into Morada at the right time in our lives and have enjoyed it every day.

I love to read and spend a lot of time doing that. I work with a Church quilting group. All our quilts are given to various charities.

I've been a lifelong Christian, and I'm grateful for the blessings in my life.

We have been married for sixty-two years, have two daughters and one son, all happily married. We have five grandchildren and, so far, four precious great-grandchildren.

William Robert Pahmeier.

Pahmeier is German, generally meaning 'low land farmer.'

When I was a little boy, I was known as 'Billy Bob,' abbreviations for William and Robert, my grandparents' names. I was born in Chamois, Mo, a small town on the Missouri river, my parent's hometown. Shortly after I was born in May of 1937, we moved to Jefferson City, the state capital (middle part of the state).

I have one sister, Barbara, who lives near Hartsburg, Mo. (ten miles from Jefferson City).

My school history.

My first thru third grade was in Jefferson City. Forth thru eighth, a country school outside of town. High school years in the Jefferson City public school system. Then a Junior college, Lincoln University, and finally at Northwestern University in Evanston, Il, just north of Chicago. I worked all through HS as a clerk in a men's clothing store, and through college, I worked in a print shop of Mo. Division of Health. I was working for the Phillips Petroleum Company in Bartlesville, Ok. when they sent me to Northwestern University for Advanced Studies in Economics.

I have always enjoyed singing, mainly in choirs and quartets, with an occasional solo. Outdoor activities over the years have included hunting, fishing, and later, a lot of tennis.

My dad had a 1937 Chevy, kept it in the barn, and maintained it in good shape after he stopped driving it, for me, as my first car. When I was a kid, I had an injury to my left kidney while playing football with some of my buddies. It was severely injured and eventually had to be removed, so when I went for the physical to join the service, I did not pass. Thus no military service for me.

I had just changed jobs from IBM to Phillips, working in Kansas City, Kansas. My wife, Katherine Sue Viats, was a grade-school teacher there, and we met at the drive-in movie at the snack bar during intermission. We recognized each other but had never been introduced. We hit it off right away, and the next week I asked her out for a date. Sue is a year younger. She went away to college while I went back home to Jefferson City, where I enrolled in two local colleges while also working. After college Sue became a grade-school teacher there in Kansas City, Kansas, yet we stayed in touch and dated when she came home to Jeff City.

It all worked out, and we married on January 1, 1960. We have three children: Kathy, living in Bartlesville, Beth in OK City, and Eric in Southern California. Kathy retired as an accountant. Beth retired as a school teacher. Eric has a pool service company near San Diego.

My first job after college was with IBM for six months. Then I resigned and was hired by Phillips Petroleum Company as a Petroleum Marketing rep to service stations in Kansas City and Indianapolis, and later on various assignments at their Bartlesville home office.

Our family always took a summer vacation trip. Quite often, it was back home to visit family. Later, as the children got older, we made more sightseeing trips. After we retired, Sue and I traveled extensively, mainly in all but two states in the northeast. We also traveled to Europe and New Zealand.

As I mentioned earlier, Sue was a grade school teacher in a Lutheran school in KC. I belonged to a different Christian denominational church. I thought it only made sense to join her church since she was a teacher there. We have remained Luthern for our entire married life of 62 ½ years.

Regarding retirement experiences, I kept up the Bass fishing hobby for many years. I have owned various boats, the last two specifically designed for Bass fishing that I used in local tournaments. Retirement experiences have mainly been traveling throughout the US, some in England, Spain, Portugal, and New Zealand. Our son lives in southern California, north of San Diego, so we have spent a lot of time during the winter at a resort about halfway between LA and SF.

We moved into SAE/Morada Feb 2022, and we both agree it was the right decision at the right time.

Raymond Earl Perkins.

I was born on February 16, 1922, in Pittsburg, Kansas, but raised in Parsons. When I was interviewed for my story, I said Yes, I'm 100 years old.

Living in the depression as a child, my mother taught me how to grow a garden to give to those who had little, prepare what we had, and be content.

In the third grade, the principal had a room where we made new rugs out of old torn-up carpets. I remember when one boy tried to jump out of the third-floor window.

I went to East Jr. High, where the civics teacher taught us how to be a gentleman. During those depression years, one neighbor was living on beans, another neighbor on peas. My mother sent me to get 25 cents worth of round steak, which she would pound the hell out of it to get it tender. A favorite thing of mine was to shoot rubber bullets made from inner tubes using a clothespin as a slingshot.

On the night before the Fourth of July, a buddy and I would sleep outside, so we would be the first to be awake when the sun rose and then shoot off firecrackers to wake everyone up. I would take my wagon full of newspapers to junk yards to get a nickle.

Every year my mother would plow the garden as a horse pulled the plow. I told mom I could do it for $5. No horse and plow, just a shovel, digging three to four rows at a time. In the summer, living in the basement on canned goods was cooler. My first paying job was delivering ice cream.

I graduated from High School in 1940 with 31 credit hours of college math with an IQ of 128. Then I went to Jr. College in Parsons, Ks. to study Math. I enlisted in the Air Corps at Coffeeville, Ks, and was sworn in on October 24, 1942, at Ft. Leavenworth, Kansas. I was transferred to Jefferson Barracks, Mo., for basic training and then to Lincoln, Nebraska, for training as a teletype operator in November. In January of '43, I was put on a troop train and sent to Pittsburg, California, via Texarkana, El Paso, Phoenix, and Los Angelos to get to San Francisco. It took a week to get there. Five thousand of us soldiers were soon on the USS Republic going under the Golden Gate Bridge heading to New Hebrides, east of New Guinea.

Several years later, they assigned me to the 13th Jungle Air Force, and because I was color blind, I was re-assigned to the 72nd Lighting Bomb Squadron. of the 5th Bomber Baron Group as the orderly room clerk typist. The color blindness may have saved my life because I first wanted to be part of an aircrew in the Army, Navy, or Air Force.

One of the clerks was sick with Malaria, and the other was off on assignment, so I studied the methods of preparing and typing the payroll. That became my job. I got promoted to PFC on June 19, 1943, then to Corporal, and on December '44 to Seargent. I was overseas from February '43 to October 13, 1945, and was discharged on October 21, 1945.

Just before the Japs surrendered, we were packed and ready to move to Okinawa on 24 hours' notice to start bombing the mainland. Did not have to go.

For the thirty-two months on the Island, I never got Malaria or Dengie fever. I told people the mosquitoes did not like me because I had bad blood. When arriving at a new base, we could always rely on Kilroy being there first. Our entertainment was listening to Tokyo Rose for good music.

Soon after my discharge, I met the love of my life, Norma, at a dance. My first car was a 1946 red Ford. Then I went to Jr. college in Parsons, Ks. to study Math. We had two children, and our marriage lasted for forty-two wonderful years together. My working career was as a Postal Carrier, from which I retired in 1981. Then I began helping others by volunteering as the soup kitchen chef at the First Presbyterian Church for seven years. In May of 2010, I started a mission outreach to Mexico in '93, as I was director of that misson for many years, also helping raise funds. I initiated a class reunion for the 1940 class at Parsons, Ks.

I resigned as Chairman in 2009. I was president of 13AF Association in 2011-2012, organizing their reunions in 2007, 2010 and 2012.

I was on the board of directors for the Oklahoma Honor Flights, which has sent over 1600 veterans to Washington

DC. While recruiting many for this trip. I volunteered and loved speaking to students of Tulsa schools about WW2.

The only overseas travel besides the time in service was to Australia for R and R and Mexico for mission trips.

I have had the belief that everyone should do some good in this world before they leave.

I moved to Morada in February 2019.

Pat Persing

Pat's Epiphany

On that long drive to Memphis the day after Thanksgiving, the early 1970s, all I could think about was, "I have a brain tumor with a 40% chance of surviving ..... What is going to happen to my two little boys? They were 4 & 5." Our first son choked to death in someone else's care, and I was literally terrified for their future. My husband & I arrived in Memphis for the first visit with the surgeon (one of 3 places in the US that performed that procedure at the time). The surgeon, being very compassionate, explained what to expect throughout the surgery and hospital stay. Once our questions were answered and the procedure scheduled for mid-January, we started that long trip back home. Having a lot of time on that drive to think about Christmas, I made up my mind to try and make this a joyous occasion (like it is meant to be), not only for my sons and husband but the rest of my family as well. My Mother had suffered a fatal heart attack the year before, and the news of my pending surgery was hard for my Dad & siblings.

Over the next few weeks, I tried to create something special for every member of my family, and no, the afghans weren't perfect (although the Christmas Candy was pretty good), but they were from my heart. During this time, thinking about the true meaning of Christmas, one day, it just came to me "The Good Lord already has a plan, and if it is my time to pass on, he will make sure both of my sons are taken care of." At that time, I couldn't describe what had transpired; I just knew that a huge weight had been lifted. I no longer worried, just focused on making the most out of each precious day I knew I had. Later, I realized that I had experienced that incredible peace that passes all understanding that only our Good Lord can provide.

The only time I almost faltered was when I had to walk out onto the tarmac and climb up the steps to get on the plane (by myself-first plane trip). I looked back at those two little boys & my husband and momentarily thought, "I may never see them again." God blesses each of us with an abundance of strength. We just need to trust in him and use the gifts he has given us. If I hadn't gotten on the plane that day, the outcome would have been much different. The tumor was not benign and had grown an inch and a half since the first test in November. Once I got through the surgery (9 hours), my recovery time was half what the doctors had predicted. The Good Lord made it possible for me to fly back home to my husband and sons five days after surgery.

My prayer had been to live long enough to see my sons become teenagers & forty-seven years later, I can say with humble gratitude, "God has blessed me with so much more than what I've asked." Sure, I had a forty-year career as a bank auditor, but more importantly, I've witnessed both of my living sons grow into true servant leaders. One who gave up a lucrative sales job with a major company to become a pastor at their church in Tulsa. The other, a criminal law professor at the U of A, has been recognized many times for his work to help every student that walks into his classroom.

I am blessed to have three wonderful grandchildren, an abundance of good friends, and many, many wonderful memories of an incredible family.

I have been and continue to be a very blessed child of God.

Background:

I was born in August of 1946 in Flagstaff, AZ. Both of my parents of Irish, Scottish, Welsh, and German descent were born and raised in Oklahoma. I have always enjoyed learning something new. My hobbies currently include needlework and reading. My first job during high school was in the local drugstore as a soda jerk. My first car was a 1976 Thunderbird Turbo Coupe (Yep —four on the floor).

My education includes the U of AR, majoring in Home Economics and Criminal Justice. Also, Graduate School of Banking at the U of WI (BAI sponsored); Graduate Trust School at the U of Chicago (ABA sponsored) and Accounting Degree by correspondence from IAS. Certifications included CBA, CFSA, CISA and CFE.

I got married in Las Vegas in 1965 (old enough to get married without my parents' permission, but not old enough to gamble??) My greatest joy while working as a bank auditor was teaching the new college graduates not only the principles of auditing, but also how the banking system works – then watching them excel & grow to new heights. Of course, my primary special interests (bringing me great joy) are my family, especially sons and grandchildren. Other interest include continuing education, St Louis Cardinal Baseball, Razorback Sports (my son being a U of AR professor). I've traveled to 45 of our states, Canada, England, France, and Italy.

I moved to Morada on May 8, 2020.

Andrew Edward Peterson

On a fall day in October 6, 1935, to be exact, I, Andrew Edward Peterson, was born to Ora Franklin and Jessie Margarite Peterson. I was the fifth of seven children. We lived in Kansas City, Mo. Went to Whittier grade school, and graduated from North East high school in Kansas City 1953.

My mom was orphaned at five years of age. My dad was one of five children. Mom was passed around until her maternal grandmother took her in. Her grandma sent her to music school, where she learned to play the piano, violin, mandolin, guitar, and most instruments. As we aged, she taught each of us how to play instruments. On an occasional night, we would open the large French window, and then the neighbors would bring their chairs and sit outside in front of our house to listen and join the singing.

As a teenager, I loved to caddy. One day I met Ralph E. Lakes, who was president of the AFL-CIO. I started caddying for him. Ralph helped me get several jobs. He wanted to send me to college, but I wasn't interested. That wasn't my forte. He asked me what I wanted to be, and I said an ironworker.

Ralph made the call, and I became an ironworker. Almost five years later, I joined the navy. I was a machinist mate second class. On a destroyer, I got to visit the western world. I crossed the equator, saw Hawaii, Midway, Quam, the Philippines, Japan, China and several other islands.

When I came home, I went back to work as an ironworker living in California.

I met my wife, Patsy Ann at Fairmont Baptist Church. We dated for some time and married on December 12, 1959. Our firstborn, Johnny Edward arrived on May 10, 1962. Then welcomed our second Allison Elaine on June 23, 1964. Johnny married and gave us two grandchildren, Alicia and Stephanie. That marriage failed and he married Michelle, who had two children.

Allison married Kevin Trent. They also gave us two graandchildren, Kary and Kourtney.

In 1985, I retired and moved to Bixby, Ok. I worked odd jobs at times, and we were active members of the First Baptist Church in Bixby. My wife Patty was a great companion. We were married for 62 years, and her health began to fail, and she passed August 2021. My heart was broken. Many people came by to help in my bereavement.

In November, I attended my church and took my violin I had been playing up until my wife died. In our opening for Sunday School, we sang some songs. I played the violin, and a lady named Dorthy McNabb played the piano. She was not used to playing along with a violinist. She invited me to come to her home to practice. She was so enjoyable. She invited me back. That was the beginning of a neat romance. We were married April 16, 2022.

We moved into the Morada Independent Living Facility. We have met a lot of wonderful people here. We have Chapel Services. We are still on our honeymoon seven months later.

Just a great new life.

Dorothy Maria Peterson

I was born to James Elbert and Martha Ellen Nelson on February 10, 1934. They lived on a Rural route in Frederick, Oklahoma. I have one sister, May Helen, who is 4 ½ years older. I grew up west and north of Walters OK. I attended several rural schools and graduated from the eighth grade at Ruth Public School. In order for me to graduate, I had to go to the school superintendent's office at the county court house in Walters and take a test. I was the only one in the eighth grade. I graduated from the twelfth grade at Geronimo High in 1951. Typing was my favorite subject.

In 1949, I met John J. Solomon on a blind date. We were married the following year, on August 16, 1950. We moved into a two-room house in Geronimo so I could finish school. We had two daughters, Cerita June and Sherry Lavone. In a few years, we started farming by leasing at first. Later, we bought 160 acres from my parents and rented an 80-acre Indian lease. We raised wheat and cattle. John drove the combine at harvest, and I drove the truck carrying the wheat to the elevator.

The girls got married, and we needed to take two of our

grandchildren to raise. Rebecca was 16 months old, and James was four years old. God also laid on my heart to invite a foster girl to live with us at the time. I raised children for 38 years. After being married for about ten years, I entered the workforce working in the proof department of City National Bank in Lawton to run a proof machine. I did that for two years until I got a chance to go to work at the Bank of Walters in Walters, OK. I worked in bookkeeping and at the drive-in window. I was there for seven years and worked up to the assistant cashier. Other jobs I had were two years at the Walters Health Dept. and three years at the Temple Greenhouse, Temple, OK.

John had COPD and Alzheimers and passed on January 26, 2004. We had been married 54 years. It took me about six months to rest and recover.

After that, I told the Lord I would go anywhere or do anything He wanted me to do. I was a member of Union Valley Baptist Church, Cookieton, OK. Before John passed, we met missionary Billie McDonald. She invited me to do things with her. We showed Billy Graham movies at the GEO correction facility in Lawton, OK. We did prayer walking, among other things at Providence, RI, and at vacation Bible School in Mexico, I taught women how to do embroidery.

Five of us grandmothers from the Cornauche Cotton Baptist association had the opportunity to spend ten days in Turkey handing out Bibles. We met a missionary/tour guide there who planned everything for us. We were called the golden girls at two different airports.

I enjoyed all of the mission work, but it was lonely when I came home to the farm. One day I said, "Oh God, I am so lonely!"

Billie called me the next week about Southern Baptist Disaster Training coming up in Lawton. She had previously taken the training, so I took the training. Within two weeks, I received a call from Disaster Relief, saying Katrina had hit New Orleans, and they were taking a bus. Billie had to babysit, but I decided to go. When we got there, our service place was a church. We slept on cots in pews and cooked under a tent. We cooked 11,400 meals almost every day by ten am, and the red cross delivered the meals.

The second day there, I was stirring a skillet (which held enough to feed 400 people), and this man was working behind me opening cans. When I got tired and sat down, he came over and sat down by me. His name was Kenneth Ray McNabb. We hit it off because he had lost his wife after a long marriage. By the time we came home in a week, we knew we would get married. We did, on February 26, 2019 at Union Valley Baptist Church in Cookietown, OK. We were married for 13 years, and he passed of congenital heart failure on September 24, 2019. At that time, we lived at the Brentwood Assistant Facility in Lawton.

My daughters thought I should live with them. Cerita had lost her husband and invited me to live with her in Bixby. I became a member of the First Baptist Church in Bixby. I was playing the piano for the senior adult department. I had been in Bixby for almost three years, and one Sunday, a man came in with a violin. His name is Andrew Edward Peterson. He and I played the music that Sunday morning. I thought we needed a little practice, so I invited him over to my place to practice.

The next is history. We were married on April 16, 2022, at First Baptist Church in Bixby. I moved in with Andrew to Morada on May 18, 2022.

John David Shoop

I was born on November 18, 1946, in Cincinnati, Ohio. I have one brother and two sisters.

In elementary school in Elgin, Ill, I was known as JD, Cave Dave, Handsome Devil. My first falling in love crush was with Emily Jones. Started to play the violin in the fourth grade. I enjoyed wrestling, climbing ropes, and playing the violin in the school chorus. In High School, I could be in the choir or play football, and that's when I heard that playing the violin was a girls thing. In the high school track meet, I competed in Pole Vault. After the third try, I took my sweatpants off to get a better jump, right there in front of the cheerleaders, other students, teachers, and the principal. Oh, was I embarrassed.

I went to the University of Illinois to major in Pre-Med., In the sophmore year, I joined the Sigma Chi fraternity but quit school during that second year. I met my first wife in college and married here in June of '66.

My first car was a 1966 Mercury Comet Caliente.

My favorite hobby was singing Karaoke and country western dancing, and watching the Senior Olympics.

Joined the Army in 1968, and sent to Officer Candidate school in Ft. Sill, Oklahoma, becoming a Second Lieutenant. And then to Ft. Benny to train as a paratrooper. On the last jump, I hurt my knees and was then assigned to Ft. Lenardwood, Mo. to be trained as a Helicopter pilot in '68, and then on to Dallas and Ft Worth. Where during part of the training, I was flying in a circle around the Dallas Metroplex. I got lost and did not know what part of the area I was in. I landed by a convenience store to ask. A truck passed me as a guy was shooting toward me.

My first overseas assignment was to Vietnam in '68. During that tour, I had over one-hundred near-death experiences flying the helicopter. As the pilot, I always made sure we did not shoot at civilians and children. After two and a half years, my first tour in Vietnam ended, and I was sent to San Francisco.

There, Hippies from the Freedom Band met me while watching a movie. Now, that's a movie to watch starring Mel Gibson: "We were soldiers once and young."

For my 2nd tour, I became a Captain and was sent to Ft. Stewart at Savannah, Georgia to become a fixed-wing pilot. Retired from the US Army after twenty years.

I've traveled to thirty-seven countries. I love to cruise and still enjoy singing Karaoke, country western dancing, and watching the senior Olympics.

I've been married four times.

P.J. Wayne

In 1933 during the Great Depression, I was born in a farmhouse near Halls, Tennessee. It was many years later, however, when I needed my birth certificate. It was then, to my surprise, I discovered my name was written as "unnamed female." At least my sex was correct. One of my older brothers filed an affidavit giving my correct name, which I had been told was chosen by my two older sisters. Now I go by the name "P.J."

My parents gave birth to six children. The first child, a boy, died as an infant.

After that, they had a daughter, two more sons, and then two daughters. I am the youngest and only one now living.

My father and mother and my four siblings had been living in St. Louis, Missouri when the depression hit. After my father lost his job and was unable to find work, he returned to the farm and again became a farmer. He grew cotton as our source of income, corn and hay to feed the livestock, and peanuts to tide us over unti a full garden produced our vegetables, and the pigs were slaughtered to provide our meat.

Wood stoves provided heat in the winter and heat for cooking and baking year-round. We drew our water from a well outside and provided light by kerosine lamps.

Our toilet was air-conditioned by fresh air Summer, Fall, Winter, and Spring. The Sears and Roebuck catalogs were our source of toilet paper. Our entertainment was provided by our battery-operated radio and our wind-up phonograph player. I did have a harmonica, but it was appreciated only by me.

It was a long walk to school, and I was not quite ready for first grade at age 5. I remember putting my head down on the table and going to sleep. It was rather apparent that I needed to drop out of school and come back when I was six.

Our family always went to church on Sundays. Since we did not have a car, we went in a wagon pulled by two horses. How well I remember the Sunday school classes. We received a big beautiful picture that went along with our lesson. It always had a verse of Scripture for us to learn. The teacher made the Bible stories exciting while captivating our attention for the entire time. We each received an envelope in which we put our ten percent tithe and checked off things that we were supposed to have done the past week.

We moved several times, first close to Maury City and then close to Alamo.

Years later, it was reported that Maury City then had one-way streets. The irony of this was that there was only one street in the town. While we were living near Alamo, several interesting things took place. My sister, who lived in St. Louis, gave me a bicycle. The only problem was that we had only grass and a dirt road on which to ride, but I rode it in spite of the challenges.

When I was eleven years old, one of my brothers gave my father a 1931 DeSoto sedan, and he taught me how to drive it. That was fun. My sister and I had to walk about a mile on a dirt road to get to the bus stop to catch the school bus. Along the way, there was a cemetery. Often on the way home, we would stop there and read the inscriptions on the tombstones. Also, along the road, were vines of wild grapes clinging to nearby trees. These little mini grapes were delicious and quite tasty. Sometimes we would go through a neighbor's watermelon patch and help ourselves to a feast of melons.

It was 1944, and WW1I was in full swing when we moved from Tennessee to Indianapolis, Indiana. There I finished Grade school, went to a college prep High school, and received an A.B. degree from Butler University in 1956. I met the man I was to marry in a Physic class at Butler, and we were married on June 11, 1955.

Our son was born on groundhog day 1960; our daughter was born in 1962. In the fall of 1960, we moved to W. Lafayette, Indiana, where my husband got his Master's Degree in Applied Mathematics at Purdue

University. After that, my husband was hired as a professor at a men's Engineering College in Terre Haute, Indiana. While he was teaching there, we moved to St. Louis for two years, where he worked on his Doctorate in Computer Science while on leave from his teaching job. In the fall of 1971, we moved to Tulsa, Oklahoma, where my husband was hired as a professor at Oral Roberts University.

Since our house in Terre Haute did not sell right away, I needed to go back to work so that we could pay for the two houses we had. Interestingly I, too, was hired at Oral Roberts University to teach in a non-major Biology Laboratory. A couple of years later, I was encouraged to get a Master's Degree at the University of Tulsa in the Biology Field.

That qualified me to get the rank of Instructor, and I taught Microbiology, Immunology (which I developed), and Research and Senior Paper.

A few years later, ORU started a Medical School which offered Graduates Courses leading to a Ph.D. in Biomedical Sciences. I entered the Program and received my Ph.D. in 1990. Since I was getting closer to retirement age, I wanted to be prepared to do something that would be enjoyable to me as well as helpful to others after I retired. Hence, I completed a Master of Arts degree In Christian Counseling in 1995, which was also the year my husband retired.

In the Spring of 1997, I had a health issue that caused me to retire. My husband was diagnosed with esophageal cancer in July 1997 and passed away in October of that year. The following four years were a time of healing, adjustment, and dormancy for me. After that, I volunteered at a Christian Shelter/Program for homeless women. I was Directory of Personal Ministry and Counseling for five years, and I loved every minute of it. Upon retiring from that, I had an office in my home where I did counseling.

My daughter had been living with me for about five years, and she had a terminal illness with many complications. In 2020 it became apparent that I was no longer able to maintain my home and care for my daughter. It was then that she and I moved into an independent senior living facility. She passed away in February 2021.

Since that time, I have continued to live in the same senior living facility. It has been a delightful and most enjoyable experience living here. I have met most of the one hundred twenty-plus residents and have developed some very dear friendships with many of them. The staff are very personal, quite caring, and always available to meet our needs. We truly feel like part of a loving family.

At age eighty-nine, I can relate to the words of the poet:

"Come and grow old with me
For the best of life is yet to be."

That's it folks.

It's been very enjoyable to put these histories together. I thank these fellow residents from the top to the bottom of my heart for their willingness and cooperation to get these stories finished and published. I hope they'll enjoy reading the stories of the other residents, as much as I've enjoyed putting them all together in this book.

Because of my hearing disability, I made notes with another resident's help as the resident related parts of their history. Some wrote or typed out their stories. I then provided each with a first draft copy for them to edit and/or change, erase or add something within their brief story.

Then I typed it and provided each a copy to get their final approval, and to keep it.

These thirty-six stories are a sampling of the total residents here at Morada, Broken Arrow, Oklahoma.

The Amazing Lord, our God, guided us all on this adventure. Thank You.

Arnold Kropp. #208 Morada, BA.

P.S. If you're looking for a retirement mansion to live in, then this may be it.